C000179220

Gettin' Poetic
on Anaesthetic

Simon Sainsbury

Clink
Street

London | New York

Published by Clink Street Publishing 2017

Copyright © 2017

First edition.

The author asserts the moral right under the Copyright, Designs and Patents Act 1988 to be identified as the author of this work.

All rights reserved. No part of this publication may be reproduced, stored in a retrieval system or transmitted, in any form or by any means without the prior consent of the author, nor be otherwise circulated in any form of binding or cover other than that with which it is published and without a similar condition being imposed on the subsequent purchaser.

ISBN:
978-1-911525-62-2 - paperback
978-1-911525-63-9 - ebook

To Carl e the Mob

Enjoy the read at my
                expence!

Simon

Dedications

I dedicate this book to my stepfather Clifford Sainsbury. Without doubt you have epitomized the word stepfather. My biological father stepped out of my life, never to be seen again and you simply stepped in to become the father I always dreamed of. Since the day you came into my life you have supported me, cared for me, loved me and made me laugh. You gained instant respect without trying to be anyone else other than yourself, and I love you for it. In a weird sort of way because of the lack of respect for my biological dad I have always called you Cliff. It doesn't change the way I feel about you, but I think its about time I called you dad.

Love you dad, from your loving son, Simon X.

I would also like to make a dedication to two friends. Without going into detail these two women share an inner strength that most people do not possess. Some are born with it, others develop it, but most use it in a way to help others, and that is what sets them apart.

To Sharon, 'The running machine'. The only thing we have in common, is we both have beautiful daughters X

And to Mel, we love you X

Acknowledgements

In Geography, I used to copy from Jock, Jock would copy from Karen and Karen would copy from Claire. I'm afraid I'm still at it! Not so much copying but copy and pasting. I know I'm rubbish with computers and I know it would have taken me forever to finish this without you, so thank you my darling for all your help and patience. (What a creep)

Someone else who has a lot of patience and who I'd like to thank is Hayley Radford at Authoright. You must have thought what the hell am I dealing with sometimes, but I am still learning the process and thank you for putting up with me being a complete numpty on the other end of your emails.

Not forgetting Gareth Howard at Authoright, who gave me the chance in the first place. I remember our first conversation on the phone and you saying 'I think you might have something'. Cheers Gareth and thank you for listening, and thanks to all the team at Clinkstreet.

Lastly I'd like to thank all my mates, not just for the material but all the great memories. Hopefully there's more to come, sorry mum.

My name is Simon, I'm married to my beautiful wife Claire and we have two wonderful children William (19) and Alice (15). I recently went into hospital for an operation on my right leg. The affect from anaesthetic left me feeling nostalgic, and I began to scribble down old memories starting from the seventies. Combined with the thirty-six hours spent in hospital and a few days after, I have turned my experience into this book. After a few pages about my youth, half of what you read about my operation was text into my phone as I saw it. I hope it comes across as intended: candid, heartfelt, honest and amusing. I also hope you like analogies because like Will.i.am, I just can't help myself. The book starts with me growing up in Tiptree and flits back and forth to present day. Most of it is flirting with danger and if you're a bit squeamish I do apologise, because I don't hold back!

Before I give you my account, I want to share with you my opinion of the NHS.

The biggest institution in Great Britain, the NHS used to be something the nation was very proud of, up there with the British Armed Forces. In recent times, however, the changes in government and the way funding has been managed have seen the NHS come under fire, scrutinised and even ridiculed by the press. Being the size it is, the NHS will never be without fault, especially when it is dealing with the health of the whole nation.

I have paid my taxes and National Insurance for over thirty years. In return, every time my family have needed treatment we have always received the best possible care. The way I look at it, doctors and nurses – much like teachers and the emergency services – feel the need to do what they do, it's their vocation. Personally I think they all do a wonderful job, and I wish the present government could resolve the serious issues they are up against. It is all too easy to jump on the bandwagon, slagging off your local hospital, and believe you me the one in Colchester is no exception. Don't get me wrong: hospitals, just like schools, have to be of the highest standards, so we must therefore try to give support whenever we can. Cast your mind back to London 2012 and the Olympic opening ceremony; did you not feel a tingling of pride watching the nurses wheeling out the beds and marching in their uniforms? Our NHS is a wonderful institution and in my opinion Danny Boyle did a fantastic job in recognising what makes Britain great. Well that's the serious bit over; I don't want to get too political.

With all this in mind, I went into hospital with hope and optimism, instead of the usual dread and loathing. If you think back, most of us have experienced at least one visit to hospital. I would guess a large number of people have stayed overnight. My first time would have been my arrival into the world. I was two weeks late and my mother said I came out scaly; which stands to reason, me being a Pisces! She also said I was just like her mum; keep everyone waiting and then make a grand entrance.

I was born in Lowestoft and raised in Tiptree, Essex. Tiptree's main claim to fame is its jam. Wilkin & Sons have been producing jam for well over a hundred years. I may sound biased here but I do believe their jam is the best around; we even spotted it on sale in a supermarket in Sydney!

Back in the seventies, along with The Anchor Press, Wilkin & Sons Jam Factory was the biggest source of employment in Tiptree.

For anyone who can remember the children's programmes Trumpton or Chigley and the six o'clock whistle, the jam factory was just like that. On the dot, at least twice a day, I can recall the factory hooter sounding off. I remember watching the factory workers hurrying there and back like robots. The smell wafting from the factory in June, though, was always a pleasant reminder that summer had started. Every year dozens of foreign students would descend on Tiptree to pick fruit. The owners even built accommodation for the students to stay in during the picking season. It was a very handy way to earn extra pocket money during the holidays, but unfortunately I couldn't resist picking one then eating one, so I wasn't going to get rich. I loved the big juicy ones and used to hate picking the scarlets; too small and too fiddly.

As a wee boy I remember my friend Hoggy's (real name Mark) mum would drive a trailer round the estate picking up anyone wanting to go strawberry picking; it was proper 'Darling Buds of May'. Hoggy's mum Mo became a Tiptree legend after she opened Tiptree's most popular eatery, Mo's Café, or as we liked to call it back then, 'Hoggy's Nosh'.

She would cook you anything and at any time of day. As a teenager I worked for a local builder called Sid, and Mo would cook us a full roast for breakfast! It used to set us up for the whole day. Oh, and her chip butties were the best! Every Christmas me and my mates would have a turkey dinner and then go clubbing afterwards. One memorable year one of the lads had a brush with death! Ada's hair caught alight after he got sprayed across the table with Silly String. The string went through a lit candle, made contact with his lacquered hair and it went up like a Christmas pudding. Luckily for Ada's sake Hoggy was sitting next to him, and with his shovel-like hands he managed to pat out the flame. Thanks to Mo's willingness to please we had a lot of fun times in her café, even if they were a bit hair-raising, boom boom! Sadly Hoggy's mum Mo is no longer with us, but her legacy lives on and the café is still going strong.

The Anchor Press attracted printers from all over the country, my father included.

We lived in a firm's house, No 19 Glebe Rd, and one of my earliest memories of Glebe Rd was sharing a bedroom with my brother Gary, who is seven years my senior. My Nan on my mum's side lived with us after my Grandad died. He passed away before my first birthday, so sadly I have no memory of him, but at least Nan was there during my early years. I expect I got spoilt more than the average toddler; you know what grandparents can be like. I have very vivid memories of Nan when she lived with us in Glebe Rd and there were always three things about her that fascinated me. First were her teeth in a glass of what I thought was soda-pop beside the bed. Second, the smelling salts in her handbag next to the obligatory packet of spangles; and third, some ultra-furry gloves that I used to think looked like bear hands. She used to stroke the side of my face with the furry side of the glove, before putting them back in the drawer. I'm not even sure she ever wore them, or if they were actually made from real fur; I'll have to ask mum. I have just thought of a fourth thing: her rain hood, it used to fold up into a square as small as a postage stamp!

At the bottom of our garden was the biggest playground you could imagine; we called it the railway track. No track in sight, but it used to be part of the branch line that went to Tollesbury. The station in Tiptree was funded by Wilkin & Sons to improve business and it stopped running in 1962. Now it's all houses! I remember it as a waste land divided into fields. At the Rectory Rd end there were a couple of sheds belonging to a local builder/businessman. He used to walk around the village with string holding up his trousers, but was reputed to be worth a lot of money and owned a lot of land in the area. In front of the sheds there stood a huge rusty old cement mixer, which had seized up. On the Anchor Road side of the railway track was another smaller shed, but this one was much harder to get to. It was covered in bramble bushes, but we managed to burrow our way in to discover a neglected vintage car. I remember it being like the one we saw in the Laurel and Hardy films; black, lots of rusted chrome and a huge skinny steering wheel. It would be an absolute dream for a car restorer, but to us it was just a great big toy. We would jump in, wipe the seats clean and drive off into the sunset. We spent hours of fun playing in that old car.

The far end of the railway track opened out to Rosemary Crescent. My friend Paul used to live in the end bungalow. A few yards from Paul's place was a big mound, and that's where you could still dig up the old track. From Rosemary Crescent to Rectory Rd there was a well-trodden grass track. It ran directly behind my house in Glebe Rd; that was the dog walkers' track. Sandwiched between the track and a couple of fields was a thick wooded area. One very uneven field was full of gooseberry bushes and in the middle of it was an enormous felled tree. We used to try and walk the length of it without falling into the gooseberry bushes. This giant playground was at the end of my garden. My friends and I made full use of it and it didn't stop there either. At the end of Glebe Rd we had 'The Ducka' (duck pond), which I'm glad to say is still there (well most of it). It comprised three ponds: one typically English pretty duck pond with an island in the middle; one rectangular very shallow pond; and then the last one was more like a bog than a pond. According to local legend, an old man died in there whilst trying to save his dog. They have both been haunting the site ever since!

Behind the bog there used to be a derelict bungalow and I remember some of my brother's friends knocking down walls with sledge hammers. Someone could have got seriously hurt, as I'm certain none of them were trained in demolition. Surrounded by horse chestnut trees, 'The Ducka' was a great place to play. It had enough space to play football, cricket and of course hares 'n' hounds. The football and cricket matches were a bit tricky because of the bush in the middle, but a huge horse chestnut tree made hares 'n' hounds the ideal game. The middle of the tree could seat at least six of us comfortably!

As a child, I constantly came home covered in mud – ripped jeans, scabby knees, cuts and bruises; a proper boy. Mum was used to it; nothing too serious though, until I broke my arm. That was my first memory of hospital. I broke it in three places, would you believe – 'The Ducka', the park and the railway track! No, seriously, it was a bad break. My so-called friend

Michael Kemmit and I were playing in Grove Rd Park. As far as I can remember, it was the only proper park with proper play equipment in Tiptree. Obviously it's since been updated, but back then it had two different kinds of swing. A set of very tall chain-linked swings, which I remember vividly because a boy called David broke both his arms on them, as a result of swinging too high! Not forgetting of course the baby swings, which everyone tried to squeeze into and then got stuck! I remember when the new helter-skelter was installed; we were all super excited. The problem was, though, we never walked up the steps; instead we would climb up the outside or even up the slide. If you were really daring, you could even clamber up on to the roof! The park also had a witch's hat that used to spin and oscillate in every direction, a merry-go-round, and a giant sand pit, which I loved. We used play this game where you take it in turns to fake dying. Basically one person runs full pelt towards the sand pit while the snipers lay in wait on the opposite side. The objective is to be as theatrical as you like when you meet your untimely death; points awarded of course – just like *Strictly*.

At this point I should get back to the story of me breaking my arm. "Let's go play on the seesaw," I said. So off we went; you know the usual seesaw stuff: up down up down, only I didn't like doing the usual stuff. I thought it would be cool to stand up whilst my friend, being the heavier of the two, sat at the bottom. As I stood up I thrust my arms in the air and shouted, "I'm the king of the castle!" Before I had the chance to sit back down again, HE GOT OFF! The king, minus a suit of armour, somersaulted through the air and came crashing down on his left arm. Ouch! I remember not crying, but arguing with Kemmit that he had actually contributed to the accident that caused me to break my arm.

Holding my twisted arm I rushed home, which was a good ten minutes away. How am I going to explain this to mum? I thought. Once I'd let myself in I could hear her hoovering, so I shouted upstairs, "Mum, I've broken my arm." Having been in the wars many times before, my mum dismissed my call for help.

"Don't be silly Simon, go back outside and play, I'm busy."

"Honest, look," I replied.

She looked down from the top of the stairs and freaked out. I vividly remember walking into A&E and the nurses saying how brave I was, which is what they always say to kids, don't they? I was really upset though, because in order to free my crooked arm the nurse had to do a hatchet job on my jumper.

I know it's hard to believe but the same boy was responsible for breaking my friend Clive's arm too; the similarity is scary. Clive was playing on top of the aforementioned cement mixer. Before I go on, I need to tell you how big it was. To us, it was a monster. To climb it was to conquer it and climb it he did. Only no one told Clive not to brag about it once he'd reached the top! There he was like Sir Edmund Hillary looking down from the peak of Everest. What he didn't account for was a forced avalanche from Master Kemmit. Before he could plant his flag and claim it for the Empire, he was on his way down. Master Kemmit had shaken him off! It further compounded our belief that Kemmit didn't like show-offs. I'd like to say he became an orthopaedic surgeon to make up for it, but the last I heard he was a policeman, probably arresting all the show-offs! Is it possible to do time for being a serial arm-breaker?

I managed to avoid hospital, but not the Kemmit's for a while after my broken arm; something of a miracle considering I spent the next few years constantly splitting my head open. Our local doctor had an ingenious method for stemming the flow of blood. Each time I split my head open he would plait my hair together, pulling the skin so tight that there was no need for even a single stitch. This was a skill my mother found extremely useful one Saturday night. Back in the days when working men's clubs were still popular, my mum and step father, along with my friend's parents, were enjoying listening to a live band in the Anchor Press Club in Tiptree. Because the Anchor Press produced so many books, they ended up with piles of misprints. They used to throw these books into two massive skips, which we then climbed into. It was like sitting in your own private library, reclining in comfort and reading all sorts of material. I remember a particular volume of saucy books by an author called Fiona Richmond. You can imagine how wide eyed we were reading that sort of material, and at the time we found them extremely daring. The whole thing was quite an education! The only problem was they had a security guard patrolling the site and he used to frighten the life out of us. He would creep up to the skip and bang on the side, shouting, "I know you're in there." The poor old boy had a gammy leg and couldn't physically get up the side of the skip, so we just stayed there – quiet as anything, waiting for him to disappear. Anyhow, back to the night in question.

There were a couple of circular reservoirs constructed from concrete opposite the club. Boys being boys when they're bored, we decided to hunt around for anything heavy enough to make a big splash. Having stored our ammo close by, we set about hurling rocks and anything else in to the water. Not content with the size of *this* splash, the older supposedly more responsible brother of the Tiptree arm-breaker went off in search of something heavier. By this time the light was fading and he came back with a load of bricks stuck together. Thinking he was Geoff bloody Capes at the Highland Games he ran and tossed the bricks with all his might. We watched intently as the bricks clipped the top of the reservoir. A piece broke off, and thinking the rest had made it over I stupidly knelt down to retrieve it (I should have waited for the splash). I put myself in the line of fire, or in my case – rock! They all shouted but it was too late. Instead of the bricks landing softly in water they landed firmly on my head… cue panic and hysteria!

Without thinking about the contract the Kemmit brothers had on my head, I ran into the social club. The band, remarkably, were half way through singing Wild Thing by The Troggs. People started screaming at the sight of this blood-drenched boy running amok between the dimly lit tables. With my arms in front me, blinded by the blood running down my face and looking like a disaster movie, I heard mum shout, "Simon, is that you?" She must have got a whiff of the family blood, as there's no way she could have recognised me. She grabbed my hand and dragged me into the toilets, turned the taps on full bore and plunged my bloody head into the basin. Remembering what the doctor showed her, she then set about plaiting my hair like some demonic hairdresser. Our doctor – and probably Vidal Sassoon, come to mention it – would have been suitably impressed. I remember emerging from the blood stained basin, looking in the mirror and thinking I look like the long-haired lover from Liverpool, with a plait!

For us 'scally-wags', the Anchor Press became an extension to our already expanding playground. Not the safest environment for kids, but I guess we were more street wise in those days. My friend Clive, who likes to be known as Wol or Wolly, used to live round the corner. Instead of picking up the phone like most people, we had a unique way of contacting one another.

I would call in, "Gibbon," whooping as loud as I could, and then wait for the call back. Before I go on, I have to mention our UFO moment or Wol will never forgive me! I think it was the summer of '78. We were on our bikes when we spotted a disc-shaped object in the sky. It hovered for a bit and then shot off with incredible speed. It continued to do so at least two or three times before it jettisoned into orbit. Without realising, we had actually biked from one end of Tiptree to the other. Wolly used to live in Anchor Road and we used to hop over the fence at the bottom of his garden and onto an unmade road belonging to the Anchor Press. They used to dump all their pallets up against the wall and we'd build dens out of them, but not any old dens! Once we had built St Paul's Cathedral out of pallets, we would then crawl inside and peer through the gaps, watching dog walkers go by. Their route led them toward a cut between my second home, St Luke's Chase, and my third home, Tarragon Close.

We stopped building the dens after I suffered an accident. I tripped and fell on to a protruding nail; it punctured my wrist and was quite a nasty injury, but it didn't warrant going to hospital.

My next visit would have been for suspected appendicitis. I was admitted and kept in overnight. It turned out to be a false alarm and the whole experience was pretty miserable. You hear people say 'you always got a bed years ago' but on this occasion there were no available beds on the children's ward, so I was stuck with a bunch of patients who I can honestly say were ready to meet their maker. My mum did complain, but what can you do. I remember seeing all these old people with tubes and wires attached to them and it made me think of my Nan. Everyone hates the thought of a close relative going through a long drawn-out death. You hear people say they would rather be hit by a bus and go quickly, but when it happens to a close member of the family it's actually very tragic. It happened to my Nan soon after my 21st birthday; she was hit by a car and died at the scene. The only blessing was she knew nothing about it. Even though I was an adult when she died, I struggled like mad coping with the loss. Nan was an active pensioner but she did like a drink or two, and it happened outside her local in Manchester. It was a massive shock to us all but at least she didn't suffer. She was the only grandparent I knew and I miss her dearly. Her living with us during my early years meant it was a double blow for me. When my parents split up in the mid-70s she moved back to Manchester. From then on I only got to see her at Christmas and during the summer holidays. She used to spoil me rotten and every summer the pair of us would hop on a bus and go to Clacton-on-Sea. If the weather was good we would sit on the beach and build sand castles, and if it wasn't we would spend pennies in the amusement arcade. We visited the same restaurant year on year and I always had the same desert, Banana split!

I won't bore you with the details, but my father left when I was about eight and took my older brother Gary with him. I'm not certain where they went, but I never saw or heard from my father ever again. As you can imagine, it was a traumatic time for all of us and it got a whole lot worse when my mum found out he had left us in debt. Mum and I had to leave the firm's house in Glebe Road due to the rent arrears.

I remember moving into my now stepfather's one-bedroom flat in St Luke's Chase. He was such an important life-line for me and mum, and god knows what would have happened without him. As for the house! I couldn't believe it – everyone from my school was convinced this house was haunted! We used to dare each other to walk up the path – to the front door and peer through the letter box. The staircase was directly in front of you and if you were brave enough to look up, you apparently saw the devil's eyes staring back at you. I remember everyone telling me not to move there; like I had a choice! It was an old house that stood on its own, with a garden and an orchard. We lived on the first floor and I slept in a camp bed on the landing. All things considered, I actually have really fond memories of that place. I had a pet guinea pig called Gilbert who was famous for being a dare-devil. Gilbert used to run around the flat with the freedom of a cat, unlike most guinea pigs that are confined to their hutch. Gilbert was no ordinary guinea pig. When my mum and step-dad went out we made a parachute, inspired by Action Man, which we would attach to Gilbert and then drop him out of the window. My friend was at the ready just in case Gilbert's parachute failed. We tied objects to the parachute that were a similar weight and had test runs before Gilbert took to the sky. I know it sounds cruel, but he loved it. As soon as he landed he would make those chirping sounds guinea pigs make when they're really happy. I suppose a child psychologist would say that dropping Gilbert out of the window was a reaction to losing my father, but I ended up with the best step-dad ever; his name is Cliff and I love him to bits. He's still with mum after all these years and he's always been there for me. As a sign of respect for my stepfather Cliff, I changed my name from Bartley to Sainsbury as soon as it was legally possible. Eventually we moved out of the haunted house and into a three-bedroom semi in Tarragon Close, which was only about 25 metres away through a cut.

Before I move on, I have to tell about the time we called the fire engine out. I was looking out of the window above the orchard and I saw a lad who was well known to everyone in the village. The next thing that happened was hard to believe. I asked my stepfather to come and watch because he was behaving suspiciously. It was then we realised he must have primed the site earlier in the day, because quick as a flash the garden was up in flames! Thankfully the fire station was only at the end of the chase and they turned up within minutes. The lad was so audacious he actually came back to the scene and asked us if we needed help putting out the fire! We moved house five times after St Luke's Chase, and they were all in Tiptree. My mum and dad still live in the village and have finally settled down in one place. I'm so glad; I used to think we were nomads! When I look back at my childhood I think I must have been lucky not to have been seriously injured, or ended up in hospital more often. I have given you in detail some accounts of my escapades, here are some more:

Head cut open (animal bone), thanks Tony!

Head cut open (rusty old tin can), thanks Nige!

Head burn (firework fired through copper pipe), thanks Dave!

Head injury (fell off bike), twice!

Suspected broken back (shaken out of a tree; not by Kemmit!)

Suspected broken coccyx (kicked very hard up the backside by my brother)

Nearly drowned (fell in the duck pond)

Potential drowning (diving into Tiptree sand pits – deep water)

Potential food poisoning (eating chewing gum off the pavement), yuk!

Tree top climbing (timing each other to see who was the quickest)

There were always going to be situations when someone would dare you to do something silly, and unfortunately I could never resist a challenge. Apart from eating chewing gum off the ground – which now disgusts me by the way, but I do recall getting a taste for it and remember spitting out the grit whilst chewing – double yuk! In my defence, isn't it just normal boy behaviour, or was I a dirty little scrote? You can decide that one. I did say I was going to be honest! Three dares I'm not proud of and would go spare if I caught my kids doing, were: one – ringing the church bells after dark, which I don't think would happen now because they lock 'em up. Two – climbing up to the top of the fire station tower and doing something too horrible to mention; and three – I somehow managed to shimmy up a very tall flag pole to pinch a Union Jack. My mum stitched it on to the back of my parka when I was a mod. She didn't know where I got it from. I think I told her it was from a jumble sale or something. I know its theft and I regret it now, but at the time it was such an adrenalin rush, and of course I gained massive respect for being the only mod in Tiptree with a full-length Union Jack on his back. I ended up selling my parka to a lad a couple of years below me at school, and soon after he bought my scooter as well!

The only photo I have of my scooter

My wife Claire says I was feral when she listens to me talk about my childhood. I'd prefer to call my childhood free rather than feral (sounds like a proper quote). The mod phase came about after we watched Quadrophenia in our teens. We all carried it through to eventually getting scooters. Myself, Wol, Dave, Pil, Woody, Hoggy and John. "We were the mods – we were the mods – we were – we were – we were the mods!"

I did come off my Vespa in Church Road, injuring my shin; the same one that I broke ten years later. It was a busy day and lots of people rushed to my aid. Apart from the fairing bending inwards and digging into my shin, there wasn't too much damage to my scooter. Somebody moved it off the road for me and I managed to hobble to the clinic up the road. I could probably write another book on the exploits of what we got up to on our scooters. My father-in-law even mentioned the fact that my scooter used changed colour every month in his speech on our wedding day! I attached sixteen mirrors to my scooter once! I thought it looked really cool until I realised at night every time a car came up behind me I couldn't see a bloody thing! I also had it booted up from a 50cc to a 90cc to keep up with anyone who had a fizz. This made it illegal, of course, but luckily for me the local plod was about as bright as the one on '*Doc Martin*', so he didn't notice the difference.

Apart from showing off at the Youth Club one night and upending my scooter, my friends and I managed to avoid any serious injury.

Dave on his Vespa, checkout the Jam shoes

We soon progressed to cars and we did go through a mad period in the winter of '85. The significant snowfall meant that venturing too far was a no-no, so once again, boys being boys when they're bored, we decided to go sledging off the back of Dave's Talbot Horizon! A long length of rope was required; a sledge, obviously; goggles for the person at the front; and a crash helmet for the one at the back. Next requirement was anyone bonkers enough to do it! In the end we all had a go and were averaging speeds of 60mph! The location was Birch Airfield, the place where everyone learnt to drive. It was a former RAF base in the war and it had a runway just long enough for take-off… on a sledge! I'm not joking. It was like our own Winter Olympics. After hitting a break-neck speed and getting a face full of ice, you then came to the bend at the end of the runway. At that point, Dave pulls up his hand break, loses control and the two on the sledge smack into a huge pile of sugar beet. Eddie the Eagle, eat your heart out! It was a bloody miracle no one got seriously injured, and I'm running out of apologies to mum.

I went through my early twenties with no more than sprained ankles as a result of playing football regularly. I did have an industrial accident though when I was working at a chicken hatchery. After a hatch we had to jet-wash all the incubators. They were walk-in incubators, and we used to wedge the doors open to deactivate the fans. It happened very quickly. I remember laying down the jet gun and hand-wiping the back of the fan. It was the size of a small propeller and somehow the wedge holding the door open moved. The door slammed shut behind me and the fan started up. It hit me full in the face and I was thrown backwards. I fell out of the closed door and ended up lying on my back. I remember after blacking out for a minute, the blood running down the small channels in the floor. The charge hand rushed over and dealt with it really well, apart from rushing me to hospital in his car. If I'd taken a turn for the worse, I doubt he could have done much. It's always safer to call an ambulance in an emergency. They told me I was extremely lucky not to lose an eye, or worse. With stitches in my eyebrow and looking like I'd been in the ring with Mike Tyson, I considered myself very fortunate that day.

No more hospital visits until I reached the age of twenty-seven. Playing football three times a week with successful local clubs and winning lots of silverware, all came to an abrupt end one evening.

Tiptree Heath, the new leaders in the premier division of the Lumley League. Back row, left to right: Pete Brown, player manager, Adrian Parker, Mick Woodley, Kevin Painter, Danny Frost, Adrian Korndale, Vic Maynard, linesman. Front: Mark Smith, Richard Seaber, Simon Sainsbury, Pete Sorrell, captain, Chris Pipe, Ally Maynard.

I remember it all too vividly. It was a match away to Sudbury under the floodlights. I saw this two-footed thug leap out of the shadows. It happened in slow motion… both feet off the ground. He launched himself like a juggernaut with no brakes; impact – my right tibia. No amount of shin-pad armoury could stop that hooligan snapping my leg. After going through me, he almost did the same to a teammate. I lay there motionless – feeling nauseous, not from the pain but from the knowing – knowing that I wasn't going to stand up and walk away. Pete, our full back, ran over and a scuffle ensued. There was lots of shouting and pushing. I heard someone say, "He can't have broken it, he'd be in agony." Foolishly, probably in shock and to prove the extent of my injury, I picked up my leg below the knee. The bottom half flopped down like a soggy frankfurter! Around me, grown men were retching and looking like they were about to faint! I may have been unlucky that day but I'm not going to feel sorry for myself. There's always somebody worse off. Even though I'm limited to what I can do, I work out as much as I can. Before my recent op I joined a gym round the corner called Anytime Fitness. I'd like to give the team there a shout out for helping me, thanks guys. The other day I was stretching next to a war veteran on the running machine. He had a prosthetic leg and was really going for it. These guys are risking their lives for Queen and country, all to ensure our freedom. I chose to play sport for pleasure and have loved doing it. You have to take the knocks as well as the enjoyment of the game.

The injury to my leg was a clean break halfway up my right tibia (shin bone); you'll remember it's the same one I injured on my Vespa. I got a welcome visit from the lads during my stay in hospital. The ward was too cramped for an entire football team, so the nurse suggested we all went down to the day room. She showed them how to operate the bed and off we went. I was praying Mick wasn't driving the bed; not that he's a bad driver, just whenever Mick's driving anything he has to experience G-force at some point during the journey. He used to test drive for Lotus (kidding). He did have a Lotus Sunbeam, though, and eventually got a proper 007 Lotus Esprit. Away matches became very interesting; whoever drew the short straw went in Mick's car, but you did arrive long before anyone else! Anyway, once they wheeled me into the day room we could all catch up. They told me that the idiot who broke my leg had been thrown out of his club. Good, I thought; he should be banned altogether in my opinion. We had a good laugh and I was really grateful. The nurse popped her head through the door and said it was time to go. As soon as she left, the beggars wound my bed up as high as it could go; said goodbye and then left me there. I could almost touch the ceiling!

When I came out of hospital, my rehabilitation was slow. I had a titanium pin from my knee down to my foot.

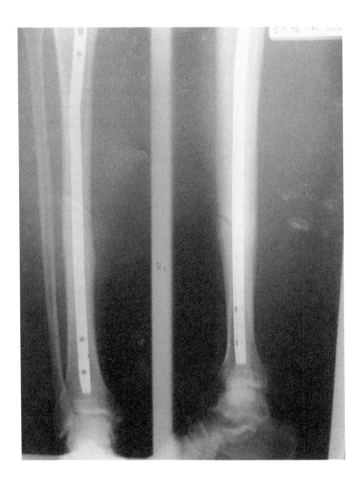

For a while I could tell you when it was going to rain! I had the pin taken out on Claire's private health insurance through the bank – I couldn't stand the rain! They told me the pin would go to somebody in the third world.

From the age of twenty-seven right through to my forties I never had much to complain about health-wise. I have to be careful with my back – occupational hazard, they say. I have been a self-employed contract gardener for the past fifteen years. The last six years I have also been a site manager for a primary school. The split shift at school enables me to carry on the gardening. The school job was only supposed to be for one winter, but they wanted me to stay on. They pensioned my predecessor off due to ill health. When I agreed to stay I had to make the decision to let half my customers go. The security the school job gives me is invaluable, especially through the winter.

As for sport, I did go back to football for a couple of seasons but was never quite the same. It wasn't the fear of tackling, but the long lay-off made my muscles weaker. Just when I thought I was getting back to normal I would pull a groin or a hamstring muscle. That hampered my reliability, so I took the option to concentrate on golf for the next few years. It is far less taxing on the body but it can play havoc with your mind. I did take a football coaching badge in my mid-thirties and went on to manage my son's team – Colchester Athletic. I really got the bug again. For a few years it took over my life. I managed, coached and became the fixture secretary. It made playing golf very difficult, what with training on Saturdays and matches on Sundays. The boys made it all worthwhile, and Claire and I gained lots of new friends through the parents. We even won the league when they were U12s. I love coaching and all my experience in football made it natural to pass down my knowledge to the next generation. I gave up coaching William after his second year at U18s and now only coach the young ones at my school. I'm pleased to say that William has followed in my footsteps and playing men's football, so many youngsters give up nowadays.

When I hit forty, I had a go at playing again. It was for a veteran's team managed by an old friend and I really enjoyed the football. It wasn't too fast and there were ex-pros and players I'd played with from years ago. Afterwards we would have a pint or two and talk about the good old days. Unfortunately for me, it was one match too many and my next visit to hospital was indeed playing for the vets. I felt something go pop in my right knee; the same leg I had broken years ago. Time to give up! It took an awfully long time to get the right diagnosis. I had a cartilage tear and had a procedure called an arthroscopy. Before the arthroscopy, the pain used to get so bad it actually made it difficult to drive. The op itself is keyhole and you're in and out of hospital the same day. After two weeks on crutches you're then ready to load-bear. Most people are back to normal after three months.

It was OK for a couple of years until the deputy head at my school – invited my daughter Alice and me to go mud-jumping.

Mad Dog May and her dog Ziggy

It's the sort of mad thing the locals do for sport; running over creeks on Mersea Island at low tide. They even have a mud race at Maldon once a year and it's huge. There are certain rules, though, like wearing old training shoes; you never know what you might land on when jumping in the muddy creek. The rest is up to you; whether you want to jump dive, or whatever. Rebekah said, "First to the other side," and off we went. It's great fun when you jump in; you get stuck, pull yourself out and start again. It is exhausting though, and a bit smelly if I'm honest, but it's also a marvellous product for your skin – and it's free! Some people pay lots of money for it in posh health clubs! When the mud has dried hard on your skin, you then go for a swim in the estuary to wash it all off. The end result is smooth glowing skin. Mind you, the glowing skin part might come from the fact that Bradwell Nuclear Power Station is just across the water!

Emily, looking radiant!

A day or two after the mud-jumping I started to get a searing pain down the back of my leg. Oh no, I thought, what have I done now? The pain, apparently, was referred, and once again I went through the same process: X-ray and physio treatment. The final diagnosis was wear and tear. The pain got worse and I kept saying it was more than arthritis. Over a year later and after a lot of pushing, they finally gave me a scan. This is where I'm going to have a moan! Why not scan first, act afterwards? It seems to be the wrong way round. Surely for someone like me, who wants to get back to work and pay his taxes, it would be more beneficial in the long run. Apart from anything else, what about the knock-on effect it has on the rest of your body? You could end up claiming disability allowance, which is far more draining on the economy.

The result of the scan was exactly what I suspected – another cartilage tear and I was booked in for a second arthroscopy. No more football and no more mud-jumping. At this rate all I'll be good for is a frame of snooker! The second arthroscopy was much like the first; the only difference being that the pain did not go away. Work became increasingly more difficult, especially the gardening. Realising I could not carry on like this, I even took matters into my own hands and bought an inversion table. The idea is you lay flat on the table, turn yourself upside down and it stretches out the spine. So there I was, hanging upside down like a bat. The kids thought it was hilarious but I didn't care; I would have tried anything. My back felt a whole lot better, but sadly my leg was still the same.

If I'm being totally honest, I thought my only option was a knee replacement. My last consultant said I was too young to have a new knee and that I would wear it out in no time doing the work I do. In the end I got referred back to a more senior consultant and he wanted to operate. Having bandy legs is quite common for footballers, but he said my right leg had become more bowed. I had no choice but to go with it. I know it sounds like I'm looking for sympathy, but surely it's not too much to ask for, is it? One mended leg and I'll be fighting fit again! Who knows, I might be able to salsa again (probably not). It's something Claire and I used to enjoy before my first torn cartilage. I have two weddings to go to this summer and I have set myself a target to have a dance at both of them, even if it is a 'dodgy dad's dance'.

Well, here goes. The day has arrived for my big op. The time is seven in the morning and my wife Claire drops me at the entrance to Colchester General. The hospital has been under review recently and has had some bad press, but like I said I'm going in there with a positive attitude. I am putting my faith in my consultant and I believe he's the right man for the job. I have a bag packed and expect my stay to be between one to three nights. Claire works full time so there's no point her coming in with me. I walk through the main entrance and continue almost to the end, but cannot see any sign for Copford Ward. I ask a member of staff, who's not quite sure herself, but she did say that if it's not signposted then it's probably upstairs. I make my way round to the staircase and ask someone else. They point upstairs but have a look of uncertainty on their face. Bearing in mind I'm going in for a leg op – it's a bloody long walk! I eventually find it and go up to the desk.

A nurse checks me in and escorts me to a bed in the corner.

I would be all alone if it were not for the gentleman next to me. His curtain is pulled half-way round the bed obscuring my view of the main desk. I look into my bag and pull out a gardening magazine that the school got me.

The school have been very understanding and on my last day the Head sat me down in front of a packed assembly. The teachers and support staff, along with the year sixes, sang me an adapted version of 'Consider Yourself' from *Oliver!* I couldn't believe it, it was so touching. After the song they presented me with a bag of goodies to help with the boredom. Kate, who's a reverend as well as being the Head, then said a prayer for me. The whole thing was a bit overwhelming and I struggled to keep it together. It's very reassuring that people care about your welfare. It drives you on and it will encourage me to get fit again.

Time – 7.20 and there's no one in sight. I get up and walk down to the desk; I spot a whiteboard with my name on and bizarrely Tina Wood, the cleaner at my school, is third from bottom! No, it can't be; she's covering some of my work (which I'm hugely thankful for by the way). It must be a coincidence. I go back and sit in my armchair beside the bed and get back to reading my gardening mag. Every few minutes I let out a cough, just to remind them I'm still here. It's now 7.55 and finally someone sees me. The nurse wants me to fill out a couple of forms and hands me a few booklets. I ask her if she knows when I'm going down and if it's not for a while could I have a glass of water? "Sorry," she says, "I'm not sure."

The thing is I was told not to eat or drink anything after last night's meal. You can sip water a few hours before but being told to come in for seven o'clock, I didn't get much chance. If I knew I was going down around midday I would have had a drink when I arrived. The time now is 9.30 and a consultant I don't recognise comes to see me. He tells me what to expect and reckons my op should be around lunchtime. I ask if I can have a drink but predictably he says no. After he's gone, I phone Claire and tell her the news.

I suppose at this point I should tell you about my procedure. It's called a High Tibia Osteotomy (HTO), or an Open Wedge Osteotomy. Basically I'm having a wedgie!

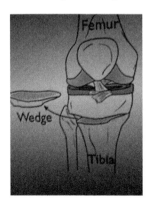

The surgeon takes a piece of bone from my pelvis and shoves it into my right leg. Apparently the stem cells in the pelvic region are more productive than anywhere else in the body, therefore encouraging the bone graft to take. To be more precise he cuts a notch in the tibia just below the knee, opens up the gap, packs it with the bone from my pelvis and reinforces it with a plate and pins. Looks like I'll be predicting the weather again! The objective is that the extra bone straightens up the bent leg. I have always been bandy and an old school friend of mine used to say I had rickets, an ancient condition usually caused by lack of vitamin D and calcium. This is where I get my own back! His surname is Pilley and the girls used to sing a rhyme at primary school which went: "Andrew Pilley had a ten-foot w…" Well – you get the drift. We did talk about joining the circus; what with my bandy legs and his you-know-what!

I haven't seen my consultant, so I'm guessing the young chap who came round earlier must be doing his rounds for him.

Not much happens for the next hour or two. The longer you wait, the more you start thinking about stuff. You wonder how you're going to feel when you come round after the op. As morbid as it sounds, it even crosses your mind that you may never come round. I know it's horrible but we all think these things, don't we? I gaze out of the window, hoping it doesn't rain too much in the coming weeks. Claire, my son William, and Nick, husband of work colleague Sonia will be covering my gardening for me while I'm off. I'm so grateful for Nick's help; he's been giving me a hand for a while now and he's one of those blokes you can truly rely on. As for Claire and William, I know they will help out as much as they can. I do have a fear at the back of my mind that this procedure may not work and I will be forced to give up the gardening, but I'm also pragmatic enough to realise that the deterioration to my leg will eventually stop me anyway.

It's now fast approaching lunch and my mouth is as dry as Gandhi's slipper. God, I could do with a drink. The nurse pokes her head round the corner only to wander off again. I don't know about you but I grew up watching *Carry On* films. I fear the temptation to say 'Matron' when I'm in hospital may overwhelm me. Suddenly, out of the blue a man turns up and says, "We're ready for you, Mr Sainsbury." This is it! The waiting is over; I'm finally going down, ooh-err!

The man throws me one of those NHS gowns, which is more like a backless teacloth held together with a piece of string! I'm now faced with a mini dilemma and wondering whether I keep my underpants on, or take them off.

The nurse pulls the curtain all the way round to give me some privacy and I start to get changed. "Are you ready?" the man says.

"No, not yet," I say, as I fumble around getting in a muddle. How can putting on a skimpy little gown be so bloody difficult? Maybe I'm more nervous than I thought I was. I finally get the hang of it and shout, "Ready," opting to keep my underpants ON. Before I could get on to the bed, the man annoyingly whipped the curtains open. I'm standing there modelling the latest Vivienne Westwood creation; a blue-and-white see-through winceyette, with my arse hanging out; very flattering!

The man then says, "Hang on," and off we go. All of a sudden I get a flashback of Mick in his Lotus! "I will get you there as fast and as safely as I can," he says. Yeah, I've heard that before, I thought.

In many ways this guy is like the warm-up act before the main event. His job is to wheel you to theatre safely; cracking jokes on the way. In general, keeping your spirits up and getting you in the mood for the big performance. We go along a series of corridors and doors, meeting patients on the way out and it felt like we were going against the traffic. Just when I thought we were going to have a head-on with another bed, my driver swerves out of the way and bursts through a set of double doors. All of a sudden we are in the anaesthetic room. I remember this place from previous operations but it still feels kind of weird; like a place you only visit in your dreams. Four gentlemen start busying themselves and one asks me my name and date of birth. It turns out we went to the same secondary school in Tiptree. We weren't at school at the same time as one another, but some of the young teachers that taught me had taught him. He asked me if I remembered Miss Mullen. "Are you kidding, of course I do; how could you forget a super-babe like her," I replied. Question! Why do anaesthetists do this?

We were just getting to the juicy bit about Miss Mullen and I drift off to sleep. It must be a power thing; knowing they can switch you off when they feel like it. Only kidding, I know it's an extremely responsible job and I'm just so grateful he jogged my memory; 'Ooh, Matron'.

Now – was I going to dream about the delectable Miss Mullen, the school's most exotic teacher, who lit every boy's Bunsen burner? Was I heck; instead of seeing this stunning teacher in high heels, I saw Mr Kazella in his football boots; with his hands down his shorts! Don't worry, he wasn't acting inappropriately, he always stood like that. I think his hands were arthritic and he was just keeping them warm. He and Mr Sprogget were excellent PE teachers.

PE was my favourite subject, so unfortunately that must be why I didn't dream of Miss Mullen, but dreams being dreams, well at least *my* dreams, I then get ejected from the spaceship in *Life of Brian*. Just before I come back down to earth I wake up. It takes me a minute or two to realise what's real and what's not. I open my mouth like a goldfish, take a big breath and almost choke on the dryness hitting the back of my throat. I swallow and it hurts, but then I remembered having that tube down my throat. The mouth that was Gandhi's slipper has now turned into the Gobi desert!

I then hear a nurse say "Water, Simon, would you like some water?" My immediate thought was; where were you at seven thirty this morning!

I replied, "Yeth, yeth pleath." I can hardly speak. She helps me sit up slightly and I take a sip. I feel like Robinson Crusoe during happy hour! Never has water tasted so good.

Powerless against the forces of anaesthesia, I then drift off again; which I think I do time and time again during the next hour or so. It's an odd feeling; you feel like you're about to come round but then this drowsiness laps over you. You submerge once again into the depths only to rise up again back to the light. You question yourself: was that a dream, or was it real?

Why is it that certain memories materialise into dreams?

Why is it that half the stuff you dream of you can never recall once awake? Just at the point before you wake up, you could be an Astrophysicist and know everything there is to know about the universe, but then as the day goes by you begin to forget it all. That's why it's good for you to meet up with old friends now and again. You jog each other's memories and then it all comes flooding back.

Anaesthetic affects people differently. A bit like alcohol; I don't know about you but I get all poetic and philosophical when I have a drink; a bit soppy too, if I'm honest. It's better than getting aggressive like some people do under the influence. Recovering from anaesthetic for me is like a squirrel coming out of hibernation. I don't feel sick like a lot of people, just cosy and warm; like I'm being cuddled. I feel content, as though I don't have a care in the world!

Before I finish my analogy of waking from anaesthetic, I move my foot and feel something at the end of the bed. What's that? I thought. I pull the sheet up from the end of the bed to reveal a crumpled pair of underpants. My underpants – that can't be right, I kept them ON before I went down.

Someone must have taken them off and tossed them at the end of the bed. All that fuss I made about keeping them on or not; I needn't have bothered. Right now I was going commando and I was in no fit state to do anything about it. Enjoying the freedom that nakedness allows, I stretch my arms above my head and wonder… who took them off?

Anyhow – back to my squirrel analogy. Please can you try to go along with it, as it's the best way I can describe it. I blame the anaesthetic! The sun rises above the window sill and caresses my face; you know the worst is over; you look forward to what's on the outside. You're ready to conquer the world; the new you – hopeful and keen. Arms stretching further like you could almost touch the sky, you then turn your attention to your supplies. Like all men, you have a little check before starting the new day and being a squirrel was no exception. I plunged my hand down to have a feel and the pain suddenly coursed through me like an electric shock! I had to investigate, so I looked around for anyone who may be watching. I tentatively picked up the sheet, drew my eyes slowly down my torso and they rested at the shadow between my legs. There was something wrong down there and I had to investigate further.

No one had prepared me for the next bit, it was bad enough seeing my underpants at the end of the bed but now it appears my willy has been swapped! Has it been spray-tanned? Look at the colour of it! I then start to panic, thinking have they made a horrible mistake; or is this some kind of sick joke? Have all my pranks come back to haunt me? Is someone getting their own back? I angle the bed-sheet toward the window to reflect the sun like a photographer's light-shade and stare at the variety of colours. Bloody hell I thought, look at the state of it! It was like the Northern Lights. Joanna Lumley would have been mightily impressed. No one told me this was going to happen! The more I look at it, the more it reminds me of a pair of tonic trousers I used to wear in my mod days. I gently lift my pitiful penis to reveal a painful pair of Technicolor testicles. The bruising is quite a spectacle; so much so, I now want to share it with someone. If I show it to the nurse, she'd probably hit it with a stick!

Honestly, losing your dignity in hospital is one thing but now I've lost all my inhibitions too. I'm desperate to show someone, me and Pilley could definitely join the circus now! It just goes to show, hospital is like golf – a great leveller. No matter what gender, race or religion, rich or poor, when we are wearing that flimsy little NHS gown, we are all the same. I know from previous experience that orthopaedic surgery can be brutal; in fact the surgeon who operated on my broken leg all those years ago compared it to woodwork. He told me how he whacked the pin into my leg with a club hammer! No wonder my leg below the knee swelled bigger than my thigh. The surgery to my pelvis must have caused all this bruising. Forget about 50 shades of grey; down there it's more like 50 shades of purple! For the first time in my life I'm actually beginning to feel sorry for myself. I let out a wounded squirrel sigh (whatever that might sound like?) and put my bruised and battered tackle away.

As I start to come round more and more I notice two people opposite: a young lad who can't be much older than my son William, who is nineteen, and a guy who looks about my age. Once again I am stuck in the corner but this is a different ward. I started in Copford and ended up in Great Tey.

A lady suddenly turns up with a drinks trolley, "tea, coffee anyone?" I immediately put my hand up and say, "Yes please." At least I can say it now (just about). She offers me a packet of cheesy biscuits (big mistake). The anaesthetic dries your mouth out so much you feel like you could drink all day long. If like me you are a tea drinker, you will understand that the first cup in the morning is the best. You take a sip and let out the obligatory sigh, followed by, "Ah, nectar." I'm a bit of a creature of habit when it comes to caffeine. I like one or two cups of tea when I get up, a coffee mid-morning, tea at lunch and a coffee after dinner. When I get out of here I'm going to give up sugar (sounds like I'm in prison); I don't want to get overweight. Even though I have tea to wash down the cheesy biscuits, I'm struggling like mad. God, my mouth is dry; it's taken me five minutes to eat three miserly biscuits. I give up; it would be easier chewing on that cardboard pee bottle sitting on the table! I notice a nurse doing the rounds and dispensing drugs. Her name is Gladys and she starts by handing out morphine to the guy opposite. I hear him say jokingly that he's hooked on the stuff. Has he wound up in hospital to keep his habit going? Surely not; it's a bit extreme, isn't it? She doesn't hand any drugs to the young lad. I think he's about to go for surgery. There are two people on my side of the ward. She sees to them before coming to me. It's like being a kid again waiting for the tuck shop to come round, although these are serious drugs and not sweets. I remember when I was a kid getting all excited opening my jamboree bag. Jamboree bags were an assortment of sweets with a toy inside, such as a paratrooper or a whistle. You always got a sherbet dib-dab – penny chews – parma violets and those red bootlaces. Today I was getting dihydrocodeine!

I ask Nurse Gladys (very apt considering the NHS is open all hours) for a pillow to put under my right buttock and 'you know where' for the pain, hoping it would give me much-wanted relief. Unfortunately Gladys declined, more or less telling me to man up, blimey she is like the one in *Open All Hours*! She told me it was referred pain and that the dihydrocodeine would soon kick in. As a protest I might show her my willy! Better not. I have to say I was expecting a bit more sympathy. Next time she comes round, I will have to work on my charm offensive. Soon after, the other nurse pops by to check my temperature and blood pressure. She's far more amiable. Her name is Keira; she's Eastern European and a real sweetie. We have a good chat before she says she must get on with her work. My aim now is to try and soften up Grumpy Gladys. Get her to smile, laugh even. I do hate stuffy quiet surroundings. I like to lighten the mood. Life's too short to be serious all the time. So many people are in so much of a hurry these days and then they become stressed and aggressive. I don't know about you but I get the feeling people are less tolerant now.

I suddenly notice Keira dropping her pen on the floor. Behave yourself, Simon, I thought. If I was Sid James in *Carry on Doctor* I'd be dropping stuff on purpose to get her to bend over, just like Barbara Windsor. Also I'd be giving Grumpy Gladys the run-around. But this is the twenty-first century; I will have to be more subtle. It's 2.15 and my consultant strolls onto the ward. He sees me briefly and explains how it all went according to plan. I thank him and off he goes. Gosh that was quick, but I know they are incredibly busy. The nurses are constantly nagging us to drink water. I have drunk jugs of the stuff and still haven't gone to the bloody toilet! Maybe the combination of anaesthetic and cheesy biscuits has soaked up all my bodily fluid. Either that or my subconscious doesn't want to pee in one of those cardboard bottles. It's bugging me what those things look like. Oh, I know now – they're shaped like a proboscis monkey nose but with a flat bottom. I guess so you can pee lying down in bed. It reminds me of a Venus flytrap for some reason, or is it one of those other insect-eating plants?

As it doesn't really have a name and I'm feeling poetic I've come up with my own; I'm going to call it – The Penis Shy Trap! I strike up a conversation with Jon opposite just as the lad next to him goes off to theatre. I think he's having surgery on his shoulder. Jon, however, has snapped his Achilles tendon. I know what a nasty injury that can be. When I used to play football regularly I used to visit a physio called John Chandler. Before working from home, he used to be the Ipswich Town physio during their glory days. He converted a bedroom into a treatment room and had pictures of Bobby Robson and all the greats that played for Ipswich. He always had a story to tell. It was worth going round there just to listen to him, as well as getting patched up for the next game. He told me how he heard John Wark's Achilles tendon snap from the dug-out in a packed Portman Road! He compared it to a violin string breaking. It makes me go all funny thinking about it.

Here's something that may surprise you. I had physio in St Mary's Hospital after my broken leg, and the physio told me that badminton was the biggest cause of Achilles-related injuries.

I ask Jon how he feels and he replies, "Great, now I'm on the morphine." I must say he looks far more comfortable than me over there – and he's peeing! In fact, now he's looking a bit smug about it, especially since I told him I haven't been. He reminds me a bit of the comedian Noel Fielding: a likable face, full of expression; a bit smug though when it comes to peeing!

Question: do you ever get annoyed when you're having a conversation with someone, their phone rings, and then they completely cut you off? I don't know about you but that really bugs me. I feel like snatching the bloody phone out of their hand and telling them not to be so rude. Well, in hospital, it's not phones but pee-breaks. I'm speaking to Jon and having a good laugh, when unbeknown to me he hits his buzzer and before you know it a nurse has whipped the curtains round his bed, completely cutting me off. There's no excuse me, pardon, or forgive me. I know they are only doing their job but it's still very annoying. I'm only jealous mind and I know it's not Jon's fault; when you gotta go, you gotta go! Anyhow peeing is like yawning, isn't it? Maybe if they left the curtains alone and let us hear or saw the relief on one another's faces, it might cause a chain reaction. While I'm on the subject, why aren't the Penis Shy Traps bigger? Ooh I'm ranting now. I don't mean bespoke ones for the size of your manhood, but what if you have an exceptionally long wee? Sometimes when I get up in the morning, I can wee for England. I'll be standing there getting cramp in my legs, thinking when's this going to end, meanwhile my wife Claire is standing outside the bathroom with her legs crossed. So I think what they should do is have a half pint and a full pint to pee in. Then you can pick the pint pot for your first wee and not worry about it overflowing. I don't think it will solve the crisis the NHS is facing, but they do say "God is in the details"

Jon's gone back to the open-plan look, which is very trendy I hear, and once again I can see his smug face. "Good wee, was it," I call. It's amazing how the nurse can turn your bedroom into an en-suite with one whip of the curtains. We chat on and realise we have a lot in common; same taste in music, same taste in food and a similar sense of humour (which is essential in hospital). If you can get on with someone in hospital, it makes the whole experience a better one.

It's time for the physios to walk round and see the patients. Nowadays they like you to get up as soon as possible. DVT is a big thing now, so it's good to get the patients moving around as much as they can. The physios eventually get to me; carrying with them a strange looking contraption, the sort of thing you'd see on *Dragon's Den*. Now let's see how their pitch is; are they going to sell it to me? I shall want at least 30% of the profits. It's not the only thing they have in their possession. Feels like Christmas; I'm getting two pressies. Not looking so smug now, are you Jon! The other gift is what they call a cricket pad (splint). It's not white like a regular cricket pad but blue (must be for one-day cricket!). It has four straps wrapped round it and the physio showed me how to adjust them. They are made from that wonderful man-made material called Velcro; you know the material that sticks to all materials. It's so sticky, in fact, that I reckon if the moon's surface was made of material, then Velcro moon-boots would be all you'd need; no amount of gravitational pull could rip you out of those beggars! Once you've built up enough strength to rip the straps apart, you need ear-defenders to stop yourself going deaf!

I have to say, I'm more interested in the Victorian baby time-machine. It actually looks like a baby-rocker with a plug on the end of it. The physios mount the device on to the bed, lift up my newly straightened leg and rest it on the cradle. They help me shuffle into the right position and plug it in. Turning one dial up and one dial down, it then starts rocking my leg to sleep. Except in my case, keeping it awake! It's a noiseless machine, so I can put the ear-defenders away for now. They show me how to operate the machine and advise me to keep it on through the night. What?! There's no chance of me getting DVT now. I have a sexy stocking on my left leg and the CPM (continuous passive motion) working my right leg. I swear I saw the full-size version in *Carry on Frankenstein*; the one that brings Oddbod to life; or was it *The Time Machine*? God, I loved that film.

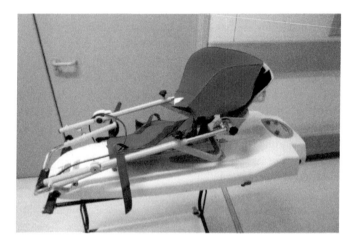

The physios leave, telling me they'll be back tomorrow to get me out of bed. Really? That means I might be allowed home; surely not?

"What the hell's that?" asks Jon intriguingly.

"A CPM," I tell him.

"What's one of them?"

I then bore him to death with my new-found knowledge of the time machine. In motion it reminds me of those nodding-donkey oil pumps; you know the ones in Texas. With a bit of luck I might strike it rich! If it gets me going in the waterworks department then I'll be a very happy bunny. If nothing else, it's quite therapeutic and slightly hypnotic. If it were Christmas they'd be able to stick me in the window as the hospital attraction. After hypnotising Jon for about half an hour, Claire and William turn up. It's so good to see them. They both give me a hug and Claire asks me if I'd eaten. I tell her about the cheesy biscuits and how I gave up on them. "I'd still be eating them now if I hadn't," I say.

"That's ridiculous, why on earth do they give you dry biscuits after an operation?" she said.

"God only knows" I say. "So where is Alice?"

"Netball," she replies. I'd forgotten she had a netball match. Alice takes her netball seriously and would never let her team mates down. I respect that and I'm sure she will come tomorrow if I'm still here. I tell Claire that if the physio can get me out of bed and on crutches, there's a chance I could be out tomorrow. She looked shocked and then asked me if I'd seen the consultant. No was my answer, but then I suddenly remembered that he did come round. I don't think I'm with it; must be the anaesthetic. Pointing at the CPM like it's a new car, I ask the pair of them why they haven't mentioned anything about it.

"What do you think of this then?" I'm getting as smug as Jon now! They looked as impressed as Graham Norton does on Eurovision night. "I'll show you how it works; you turn this dial for Radio 1 and that one for Heart Essex."

"What's it called?" asks William.

"A constant passive motion device, or CPM for short," I tell him. At that point a lady turns up with food and drink. She hands me over a corned beef sandwich made from white bread, which I didn't order, and a fruit pot. I ask William to get up and grab me a tea. As soon as he's on his feet I lift up the covers on the bed and show Claire one of the Seven Wonders of the World. Hopefully I'll get more of a reaction this time. "What do you think of that?" I say. With a look of both horror and bewilderment she then gives me some much wanted sympathy; too much for William's liking.

"Leave it out mum, that's embarrassing," he moans.

Lapping up the attention, I then show her my discarded underpants at the end of the bed. She raises her eyebrows and says, "What are they doing there?"

"I haven't got a clue," I say. She picks them up and grabs a fresh pair out of my bag. "No point, I can't get them on," I said in my wounded squirrel voice; more sympathy. At that point Grumpy Gladys turns up again with her mobile sweet shop. I go for the charm offensive on this occasion, and tell her that now the CPM is up and running my leg feels OK but I've lost the feeling in my backside. With Claire and William present it might be hard for Gladys to resist my request for a pillow. Instead there's a compromise, and she comes back with a towel and a rubber band. I place it immediately under my right buttock and got instant relief. "Ah thanks Gladys," I say. "The magic towel has hit the spot." She cracks a smile, hands me my Jamboree bag and walks off.

I know I call her Grumpy Gladys, but really it's a term of endearment. I'm sure that underneath that tough exterior there's a heart of gold. She's probably having a bad day; we all get them. I bet she's been pounding these wards for years; seen and heard it all. I'll soften her up, I've just got to pick the right time. Claire and William are ready to go but before they do, Pete in the bed next to me has a bit of an episode. The nurses whip round the curtains and you can hear the poor chap being violently sick. I see the look on William's face, like he wants to get out of here ASAP. Anaesthetic can make you sick, as can morphine. Having had a hip replacement, Pete's probably heavily dosed up. Claire gives a me a banana, a peck on the cheek and she and William leave.

I don't know why she's given me a banana. I've lost my appetite and I haven't even touched my corned beef sandwich. I shall save them for when I'm feeling hungry. I have never been one for wasting food and I rarely go off food. The fruit pots, however, are a triumph; I could eat dozens of those little beauties; they're so fruity. I cheekily asked for another. It must be the dry mouth thing that's making them more appealing. After I polish off another fruit pot, I feel a stirring in my loins. Surely not, I thought; going commando under these thin sheets is a recipe for disaster. I swear I haven't dropped anything on purpose for Keira to pick up. If that purple monster rears its ugly head, I will have to hit it with a stick, never mind Gladys! Thankfully and to my utter relief, the stirring in my loins was my bladder coming back to life. I hit my buzzer like a crazed student on *University Challenge*; in fact, as I hit mine, I hear others going off. All of a sudden it's like *Britain's Got Talent*. All we need now is Ant & Dec putting an arm of consolation around Gladys's shoulder and escorting her off the ward. Of course that doesn't happen and the nurses spring into action. They couldn't get the curtains round quick enough! Am I finally going to pee? Never has a wee been so eagerly awaited.

My theory is the CPM is acting as some sort of wheel or piston (pardon the pun); almost like a steamboat with one paddle, or piddle in my case (pardon the pun, again) Well – going with yet another analogy, if that's true then this boat is going full steam ahead and up the Pississippi! I grab the Penis Shy Trap and panic straight away, thinking, what if I have one my mega-wees? I carefully lower my two-toned tortured todger into the Penis Shy Trap (wishing it was a pint) and let out the biggest sigh. Yes you've guessed it; much bigger than the first cup of tea sigh and even bigger than a wounded squirrel! Before the nurse could pull my curtains round fully, I'd filled it up and presented it to her. I was like a master brewer showing off his award winning beer! The steam was rising from the neck like the morning mist, giving the poor girl a free facial. All she needs now is to go mud jumping with Rebekah and that would be her beauty treatment sorted for the day!

"I'm going to need another," I say. She swiftly shoots off between the curtains holding my warm wee and I couldn't help thinking by 'eck, Bear Grylls would love that! She soon came back with an empty and I half-filled that too! Now I was going again I kept an empty under the sheet, just in case. When she pulled back the curtains I was half expecting a round of applause. I sat bolt upright like a proud dad completing a piece of flat-packed furniture and having no screws left over. At last, I was one of the gang! You can't be initiated into the gang unless you have filled up a Penis Shy Trap. Isn't it mad how happy you get over the silliest things? I've got mixed feelings of joy and paranoia.

Jon opposite gives me the nod of approval and says well done, like it was a huge achievement peeing into a cardboard box. The problem is that while everyone else has been peeing all afternoon, my bladder has now reached the size of a space hopper! Now it's like someone has punched a hole in the Hoover Dam. All of a sudden I've got this horrible thought: seven jugs of water are about to cascade out of me like a tsunami! Was I going to get washed away, clinging desperately to my CPM, which I've renamed Constant Pissing Machine, by the way? Or was I going to end up back in the aptly named Cop-Ford ward? Whatever's going to happen, I doubt if I'll get any peace until I'm completely drained of all bodily fluid. Maybe I'll have to finish off my cheesy biscuits to soak it all up! One thing I have decided: I'm done with hitting the buzzer every time I want to pee, and Jon also thinks it's a good idea. Apart from anything else it's disruptive when you're having a conversation. I'm sure the girls will appreciate us leaving them alone for a while. They must feel more like Bavarian barmaids than nurses!

Oh look, the young lad has come back from his op. Jon and I quiz him about it and obligingly he tells us that this is his second op in four months. The next bit is one hell of a coincidence. His name is Daniel and he was injured playing football when he went running towards goal at speed and collided with the goalkeeper. He explained how the keeper was at least six foot, which is pretty tall considering it was an U17 match. Anyhow they both ended up in a heap on the ground, with him coming off a lot worse. He then went on to say the keeper's mum had first aid training and dealt with the whole situation brilliantly. Then I remembered my sister-in-law telling us how her son Andrew had a nasty collision playing for his football team. I ask Daniel who he was playing for and against whom.

"Oh it was Layer, and I play for Oyster from Mersea."

"Well I never," I replied. "That goalkeeper was only my blinking nephew."

"No way," he says. "Thank his mum again for me, won't you."

"I'll text her now, she'll never believe it." It certainly is a small world. Four months ago this seventeen-year-old boy had metalwork put into his shoulder after clattering into my nephew and now he's back having an artificial bone graft.

"Is that it now, op wise?" I ask him.

"Hopefully" he says.

I text my sister-in-law, then somehow get on the subject of names and after we have a laugh over my middle name Hilliard, Daniel says "You'll never guess mine." His surname is McShane, so we come up with the obvious one – Ian, the actor; the one who used to play *Lovejoy* in the TV show, about an antique dealer. After getting nowhere, he tells us it's Shane; Shane McShane! Sounds like another dodgy antique dealer! Within minutes I get a text back from my sister-in-law Lisa, sending her best wishes. It dawns on me that Shane McShane, Jon and I have all ended up in hospital as a result of playing our national game; not much of an advert, are we?

It's now about nine in the evening, Gladys and Keira have swapped with the night-shift and we get on the subject of sleeping, mainly because Pete next to me has started snoring. I don't begrudge Pete snoring, as he's had a bit of a rough day; unlike the time when my daughter stayed in hospital. Like Shane McShane, my daughter had to go back for a second operation. She's had another skin graft in her ear drum, because the first wasn't successful. Without the op, she could have lost the hearing in her right ear. We think it all started when she picked up an ear infection in Turkey. For the past four years she has worn an earplug every time she has a shower a bath or goes swimming. She was in the children's ward in this very hospital and it was approaching bedtime. The ward was relatively quiet, until the mother of a patient decided to go to bed before any of the children. You're allowed to stay with your child on the children's ward, but what I found to be completely selfish and totally inconsiderate is this damn woman had the loudest snore I've ever heard. Alice found this hysterical, which it may have been initially, but after twenty minutes or so it was like living next door to a building site! I swear I could see the false-ceiling tiles vibrating. In the end I got up and went to the ward desk. I asked the nurses to listen carefully so they could hear this woman in all her pneumatic glory. Bearing in mind the main desk was a good twenty metres away, they could still hear her! In disbelief the nurse followed me round to where the beast lay.

"Can't you wheel her out of the ward?" I suggested.

"It's one option," the nurse said but she decided to give her a polite nudge instead. The beast grunted, snorted, turned over and then stopped. For one minute at least silence fell upon the ward; it was lovely. We looked at each other like we knew it was too good to be true and then like an old tractor starting for the first time after a hard winter, the beast fired up once more. This time it was even louder and ready to plough on all through the night. Luckily for Alice she had packing and a huge bandage over her ear, so at least she could bury her other ear in the pillow.

Back on my ward and Pete's snoring is only Conference League compared to the 'beast of children's ward'. I tell Jon how it reminds me of the Lenny Henry advert and how we have always stayed in his hotels. "Never had a bad experience in Lenny's," I say; unlike the other budget hotel we stayed in, in Chichester. What a lovely place Chichester is, but they need to get rid of that awful hotel. I went to bed on one of those put-you-up thingies. I woke up in the middle of the night soaking wet! I thought I'd left a window open but then realised you couldn't open the windows, as they were fixed shut. The rain was actually coming through the top of the frame. The room was very dated and we didn't think much to the breakfast either. We vowed never to set foot in another after that day.

I know one thing is for sure, I don't think I'll get much sleep on this ward if I keep peeing all night. Ever since I started I can't stop; I'm beginning to think I'm rigged up to the bloody guttering! The night nurses will soon get fed up with me hitting the buzzer every time I want to pee. I can see why they separate the wards according to sex. Don't get me wrong, I love women;

I work in a school full of them, but when you're looking your undignified best, you're better off being with your own sex.

It's now dark outside, the windows are open and there's a nice cool breeze gently passing through the ward. I often think hospitals are too warm and too stuffy, so it's a welcome relief to be by a window. Jon and I are still chatting and I'm beginning to think we should call it a day. You know when you're enjoying yourself in a pub and the landlady wants to clear up and go home; well, I get the feeling the nurse might say something soon. I think I'll just sneak another round in before she calls last orders. Once again I manage to fill up another PST and being the benevolent person that I am I give the night nurse another free facial. I hand it over to her very carefully, like I'm handling a bottle of liquid nitrogen. Like I said before, when it's so full, and because of its shape, you can't sit it flat on the table for fear of it over-flowing. I mention to the night nurse that I should have a cabinet beside the bed full of empties; in two different sizes of course. That way I wouldn't have to bother her. I don't think she found it very funny, or a good idea, because she walked off mumbling something. Oh well you can't please them all. Mainly because she didn't laugh at the joke and to keep Jon entertained, when she was out of earshot I said, "See that nurse, she's taking the piss!" He shakes his head and without saying anything we telepathically call it a day.

The nurse comes back after a couple of minutes of silence and says, "If you like I can switch on the reading lights above your head." For one second I thought she was going to say, "If you like I can wheel you over a piss-pot cabinet!"… Well come on – it has been a long day.

Jon said yes to the light, by the way, but I declined. I've got so much pee coming out of me, sticking a light above my head will only make me look like a Charlie Dimmock water feature!

Before I shuffle myself into a conspicuous sleeping position I utter the words that I've been longing to say since I was a little boy watching *The Waltons*; "Goodnight Jon Boy." I shut my eyes and the silence is deafening. It's amazing how your ears adjust to their surroundings. You begin to pick out noises from the ward next door; owls hooting outside and cars from the main road. Pete starts to snore again, which is good, as it might drown out the sound of me peeing. Surely this is it now; I must be drained of all bodily fluids. By the morning I could be just a pile of skin! The nurse walked by, so I didn't have to buzz this time. Jon's reading, and I'm wondering whether I have enough material to possibly write a book. I'm no academic but I do enjoy writing poetry. I'm not prolific, more occasional, like birthdays, anniversaries and so on. I do admire and appreciate authors who can conjure up stories from their imagination but I prefer writers who write the truth. Somehow the truth in a book resonates with me, it's much like a photo; a moment in time, the here and now, I'm just describing what I see and hear. If this does turn into a book, it will be a miracle. I will just be happy if people can relate to it, find it funny, and it makes hospital more bearable. If nothing else it's something I can leave to my kids and failing that someone might actually come up with a proper name for a cardboard piss pot. I'm probably showing my ignorance here; is there already a name for it? There is, isn't there; oh well, I don't really care. I'm going to leave it and go to sleep. The CPM is starting to hypnotise me and I'm yawning like anything; I'm slowly drifting off. I hope I don't dream about Mr Kazella again! No hard feelings Sir.

Sometime in the middle of the night, god knows what time it is, I wake up in the most awful pain. I have to get my leg off this CPM. The more I try, the more the pain increases. I lay there in agony, for what seemed like an eternity. I don't want to wake anyone up, or cause a fuss. I can't reach my phone and I can't see the clock on the ward, because of Pete's curtain. I can't bear it any longer, I've got no choice; I have to hit my buzzer! The nurse comes over immediately and asks what the matter is. By this time it's so painful I can barely speak. I point to the CPM and mutter, "Off, please get it off." She lifts my leg, which sends me through the roof. The pain is not in my leg but my hip (the donor site in my pelvis). "I need to get up," I

54

say, so she grabs the cricket pad and lays it on the bed. As I'm putting the cricket pad on, I may as well use a cricket analogy. I feel like a rookie batsman's first time out at Lords. I frantically rip the straps apart.

The noise from the Velcro has now woken up the entire ward, but like the 'beast from children's ward' I don't care. All I can think about is getting rid of this awful pain in my hip. Somehow I have to stand up. With the pad now in place I am ready to take to the crease. It takes all my strength, as well as the poor nurse to get me on to my feet. The problem is, once I get there I can't move. I am rigid with pain and I daren't move a muscle. The nurse offers her hand and tries to move me but I am stuck in a rut and as stubborn as Geoffrey Boycott playing for England in a five-day test match. They say true cricket is test cricket. Well, this certainly is a test for anyone.

The poor nurse is surplus to requirements. I stand there not budging for at least twenty minutes, with not a run in sight. The only contribution she can make is to either pick me up from the floor after a Yorker, or to call a drinks break. We decide on the latter and after my morphine-induced drinks break, I clamber back to the pavilion and into bed. I apologise profusely for being out for a miserable duck! She says, "Don't worry about it, it's my job," and then gives me a great big smile.

I feel pathetic and ashamed having wasted half an hour of this poor girl's life. These nurses really are angels! I lay there in bed with the morphine kicking in. I look at the CPM with disdain. For me, man and machine's love affair was over!

Early next morning – barely light – I'm awakened by a beautiful dawn chorus. It's so peaceful. Calmed by stillness and the fact I am still under the influence, I lay there listening to the birds. They are the only sound I can hear and it's heavenly. Everyone else is still asleep; the street lights are still on outside and I'm guessing it's about four o' clock. I reflect on the horrendous night I had and hope it won't happen again. Somehow my hip must have got locked up, or the CPM was just too much straight after the operation. I pull myself up in the bed and stare out of the window. You get a good view from here. Probably not good enough for the old boot in *Fawlty Towers*, but it's good enough for me. I can see 'Jumbo', the water-tower. It's a rather splendid building, constructed mainly of red brick. It's named after the famous elephant at London Zoo. I think it was a derogatory comment back in Victorian times, but now the building is loved by the locals and without doubt a Colchester landmark. One day someone will do something with it. It's had various owners but no one seems to be able to cut through the red tape. I do wonder about planning laws sometimes. Why not let someone restore an ancient building to live in or open as a restaurant for the public to enjoy, rather than let it go to rack and ruin.

The other landmark you can see is the Town Hall; another resplendent building, which towers above the high street. At the very top of the tower is a statue of St Helena – Colchester's patron saint.

History lesson over, folks! Slowly it begins to get lighter. The birds are competing like its *X-Factor*. It sounds like a big mash-up of musical talent. I recognise a few songs but I'm not going to kid myself thinking that I'm Bill Oddie. What happened to Bill Oddie? I do hope he's all right. I heard he got released from *Springwatch*. I don't think he did a Clarkson and lamped someone, but I'm sure he didn't go quietly. Whenever I watched it I thought he was really good, I liked his relaxed approach. You can tell he's passionate about wildlife. I actually bumped into him once at Colchester Zoo when William was a toddler. I have to say I do have a soft spot for him, having grown up watching *The Goodies*. Now that was a funny show; I wonder what happened to the tandem? More to the point, why don't I watch *Springwatch* anymore? I used to watch it all the time. Somehow you felt a better person for watching it; a bit like reporting a crime. You feel cleansed through watching wildlife.

I appreciate the countryside and I love being outdoors. In fact, if I ruled a dictatorship I would make everyone watch it! At my school they have this thing called Forest School and it focuses on developing confidence and self-esteem through hands on learning. In our case we had Essex Wildlife Trust come into our school and teach the kids how to connect with the great outdoors. The children learn how to build dens, make instruments from wood, sit responsibly round an open fire, and they absolutely love it. So any parent who's got a child sitting at home vegging in front of the telly or floating around in cyberspace – get them outside and appreciating nature, they will be a lot better for it. Then when they have exhausted themselves and you, they can then watch *Springwatch*. After all that, it should leave you feeling Humble. Now there's a bird of paradise! "Ooh, Matron." Oh god, I've said it again – what a carry on!

Right now I am the only one awake in the Great Tey plaza and I need to get to my phone, so I pull myself towards the table. I started texting into my phone but have now realised I've used up all of my text allowance. If this has got any chance of being a book, I shall have to start using a pen. In the bag of goodies the school gave me is a note pad entitled 'Simon's Prank Book'; I can use that. I can't believe they actually encourage me to prank them at school. They thought I could fill the pad up with pranks that I conjure up during my convalescence.

I have to confess one of the best pranks at school was when I found out my head had bought a brand new clarinet. There it was in its pristine case in her office. I had strict orders to go nowhere near it – which is like a red rag to a bull. She was covering a year six lesson and sent one of the children back to the office to fetch her new instrument. When the child gave it to her she said to everyone, "I'm going to show you my new clarinet." Proud as punch she opened the case and there sitting in its place was a decrepit-looking recorder. She knew straight away it was me, and sent the same child to find me. I know it's cruel but I got a heap of kids on April Fools' Day a few years ago. I put a board up outside the school entrance saying a member of One Direction would be coming into school to talk about fame at a young age. The word got around and a load of mums were wetting themselves with excitement. A lot of people were very disappointed that day and I'm truly sorry, honest.

After last night's episode, I'm not sure if they will let me go home today. I'm not sure I want to go! If my hip plays up like that again, hospital seems like the only option. Jon is having a good sleep. I feel a bit sorry for him after he said he'd been sleeping on a friend's air-bed. Like me, Jon works for a school. He looks after children with disabilities. I'm not sure I could do it. As much as I love helping and coaching children, I think I'd find it too distressing. We have a friend who has a daughter the same age as Alice. She was born with a rare condition called Rett syndrome. It mostly affects girls and is extremely rare in boys. The brutal thing about Rett syndrome is it usually goes undetected for the first few months. The parents then begin to notice their child's development slows down. It's a brain condition that can cause severe physical and mental disabilities. It takes away their childhood and traps them inside their own body; they cannot obey signals from the brain, like you or I can. My heart goes out to our friend and other parents affected by this condition.

I don't know whether Jon has any children with Rett syndrome but whatever their condition, it takes a special person to look after those kids. It really does make you thankful when your own kids are healthy. Health really is the most important thing in our lives, is it not? Now there's a question! What if I said – you could live a healthy life, but without love. For me, to love and be loved is more important, otherwise all these incredible parents would not devote their lives to their handicapped children. They love their kids unconditionally, just like we all should!

My goodness, waking up at the crack of dawn makes me all philosophical too; like when I've had drink. Perhaps I'll turn my attention to religion. I wouldn't know where to start! History proves that religion can kill or cure. Faith is a powerful thing but when a man's love for his faith is greater than mankind itself, it's a recipe for disaster. I still maintain love is the answer to a happy life, but only when it's focused on more than one person. If you only love one person, or one thing, then it's an obsession and an obsession isn't healthy. Of course, this is my opinion. No one really has the answer to a happy life and if you live a long life, it's virtually impossible to be happy all of the time. What about the people who have lived through wars, witnessed atrocities or been forced into slavery? What about all the refugees? There are many victims in this world and the only way I can make sense of it all is that the perpetrators who inflict misery on others do not understand the meaning of true love.

Getting all philosophical has the tendency to make you think too deeply and sometimes thinking too much, or over-thinking, can be detrimental to your health. You hear about depression and how it affects the deep thinkers. Digging too deep into your thoughts can dredge up dark images. For me, I'd rather keep above ground. My mum and dad split up when I was young and I'd rather not go potholing looking for answers. You can't change the past, and the only person who can answer the one question I have ever had is my father. He died a few years ago, so I guess I shall never know. Gosh, that was all getting a bit heavy, was it not? Time to lift the mood I think.

Looks like the night nurses are going home already. No disrespect to them, but I'll be glad to see Keira and Gladys back on the ward. The Great Tey plaza will be back to normal. The lady comes round with the breakfast orders. I choose cornflakes and a cup of tea. Hopefully the tea will arrive first.

Jon's awake and we exchange a morning greeting. "What happened last night?" he says.

"Sorry mate, I had a bit of a rough time." I go on to explain the whole embarrassing episode and how that poor nurse could do nothing for me. Was I pleased to get that morphine inside me, I tell him. "That nurse probably thinks I'm a right wimp."

"Nah, I could hear you were in pain," says John.

Gladys and Keira do their usual rounds; Gladys's mobile sweet shop is back in full swing and Keira raises your blood pressure first thing. I manage to keep mine under control and she tells me it's good.

"I wonder what it was like last night," I say. I go on to tell her that I'd got myself into a bit of a state.

"Oh, you poor thing," she says. You can always rely on a bit of sympathy from Keira; she's such a darling. Gladys doesn't seem so grumpy today. I knew she was having a bad day yesterday, unless she heard me complaining about her to Claire. No, I'm sure that's not the case; I'm going to give her the benefit of the doubt. Besides, I wouldn't be so vain as to think she'd change for my sake. We are all entitled to have a bad day once in a while. You can't smile all day long; only the Queen can do that!

There's another nurse I don't recognise on the ward today. The nurse and two of the physios have pulled the curtains round Pete's bed but I can't make out what they're saying. Then I hear Pete saying to them that he's not ready to go home. I can't imagine they would be pushing him to go. As hard as it is to believe there's been a spare bed on this ward ever since I've been here. Maybe he doesn't want to miss tonight's bingo! (Kidding) Given the choice, I'd sooner miss the bingo and go home but I have got to get up on my crutches first. If Jon can do the same, we could both be out of here by the end of the day. We may not get the chance to see the pool on the top floor. I know that Shane McShane is leaving this morning. That would mean Pete and his neighbour get the Great Tey plaza to themselves.

After Pete gets his own way, Jon and I start to talk about going home and the difficulties we might have. I tell Jon there's no way he can go home if there's no one to look after him. That's the first question they ask you. He has been talking to his son, who's in the RAF. He's hoping that he can get some leave and come and look after him. Pete and his neighbour will be fine; I've seen lots of family visiting. You need support when you're convalescing; none of us are going to be walking around for a while.

Claire has already said that she's going to pop home every day for lunch. I'm extremely lucky that she works for a school just round the corner. If you can walk or cycle to work, it's a huge bonus. Also it saves you money in travelling expenses (state the bleeding obvious). Normally I'm a very active person; I'm fifty now and apart from my dodgy leg, I still feel and weigh the same as I did in my twenties. I understand that the procedure I've had could improve the quality of my life and I don't want to jeopardise my chances of a full recovery. I've resigned myself to the fact that for the first few weeks I can do nothing apart from the exercises they give me. I've watched the operation online and done my research and although each case is different, I like to think that because I have kept myself in good shape my recovery period will be minimal.

I invested in a good telly and a music system about four years ago, so I'll be listening to lots of music. Perhaps I might even watch daytime telly. One thing is for sure: you won't catch me watching *The Jeremy Kyle Show*. I know it's hugely popular, but I can't see what's great about watching families warring on TV. To me it's like watching a bunch of kids on too many E-numbers. I shall have to record *Sunday Brunch* and watch it through the week. Cheers Tim, cheers Simon. There's always *This Morning* of course, at least it's topical and entertaining. How often do you get to discuss something as sensitive as depression one minute, then talk to someone who lives and sleeps with life-sized dolls the next; hats off to Phil and Holly for keeping a straight face. Mind you occasionally you do see them lose it and off camera they must be wetting themselves half the time. Honestly though they really do make it look easy. One thing I do make a habit of watching when I'm around at lunch time is *Bargain Hunt*. I have always liked antiques and the format of the show means anyone can have a go at being a dealer. It's a lot easier, mind you, when you're spending someone else's money! Also it gets quite exciting when it's auction time. Some pieces sell for a terrific amount of money, which the contestants then get to keep, of course.

If I won the lottery I'd have an ultra-modern house with really expensive antiques dotted around. I love the mix of old and new. That reminds me of a customer I once had. A dear old gentleman called Brian. I went to his house to give a quote for his garden; I got the shock of my life when I met him, not to mention his wilderness of a garden. He opened the door looking very distinguished in a tweed suit and tie. He was the sort of character you'd see in a David Walliams book; softly and well spoken, with clipped tones from a bygone era. As he spoke I couldn't help but notice the dog hairs floating from his head and shoulders; he was covered in them! My nose started to twitch, so I discreetly shuffled back a step. He was telling me about the back garden and how it had been neglected for quite some time. I found it extremely difficult to concentrate, as I was tracking each and every hair floating from his person.

I could tell from the state of the front garden that this was going to be a mammoth task. He invited me through the house to enter the back garden. It was a long hallway with doors left and right. The walls were littered with cuckoo clocks and those too were completely smothered in dust and dog hairs.

It looked like a scene from a Harry Potter movie. Brian led the way and I followed – holding my breath. For a split second I felt like I was in another film (*Indiana Jones and the Temple Of Doom*). Then all of a sudden, I got the fright of my life! It must have struck the hour, because simultaneously all these cuckoos started attacking me! At least, that's what it felt like. Every single bird seemed to shoot out a handful of dust. I was half-expecting a giant ball to appear round the corner as we entered the kitchen!

"That's a lot of clocks," I exhaled.

"Yes, my passion is antiques," he said.

The kitchen, I'm afraid to say, was as neglected as the garden. Sitting in the doorway to the outside was his dog; an English Shepherd with the widest eyes I've ever seen. It looked rather ill, or it had been on ecstasy all weekend. He shooed his dog out of the way and stepped outside. Never have I been so pleased to breathe fresh air. I stood in his wilderness of a garden, thinking, what the hell am I doing here?

Brian offered me a cup of tea but I declined for obvious reasons and told him I'd just had one at my previous customers. He told me that somewhere in the garden was a pond, a rockery and a lawn. All I could see was jungle!

I spotted a laburnum and a silver birch but I wouldn't have been surprised if I'd seen a silverback and a python! That was the point when I should have cut and run but for some reason I didn't. He kept apologising and saying it was a huge job and he would completely understand if I said no. I'm not sure if I was up for the challenge or just soft in the head, but I reassured him that I could get his garden back to its former glory. He shook my hand and seemed extremely happy. I went once and sometimes twice a week for a whole year and eventually got the garden back to how it had once looked. I had to do so much cutting back, especially to the Russian Ivy; no wonder they call it mile-a-minute. That plant is really from another planet! I planted shrubs and perennials; re-seeded the lawn; cleared the pond; and he was absolutely over moon. I cleared van-loads of vegetation out of that garden, and even gained next door as new customer. The neighbour was just as happy, as the jungle was beginning to engulf her garden as well as his. As time went by I grew very fond of this eccentric old gentleman. He asked me to do him a favour once and dig something out of his shed. The shed wasn't your normal wooden shed, instead it was a big brick-built thing; solid as a rock and dry as a bone. He said that inside were some garden tools that he hadn't clapped eyes on in years and then went on to say, "You have inspired me to do a bit of gardening, there is one slight problem though, it's rather full of paper!" He wasn't kidding! I opened the shed door and an avalanche of newspapers fell on top of me. Basically he hadn't recycled any papers for well over a decade. He had a *Gazette* and a tabloid paper delivered every day and once he'd finished reading them, he chucked them in the shed. It took me half a day to get rid of that lot; all for the sake of a pair of loppers, secateurs and some shears. After all that effort at least I persuaded him to recycle, but it didn't take him long to fill up the shed again with collectables

Another favour he asked of me was to move something in the house. He couldn't run a bath because it was full of a 00-gauge Hornby train set, unboxed!

"I need to find a home for it other than the bath," he said.

Well – it was so comical. I had this massive pile of track and train carriages in my arms with Brian wandering round his house. We were looking for a space for it all; space being the operative word. We tried the living room but that was completely full of collectibles (stacks of 45s as high as the ceiling). Everywhere we looked there were piles of antiques. Eventually – after trawling the house – I put the train set in the only available space; the bottom of his bed!

Restoring the garden definitely inspired Brian, because he did start to keep his house in order. Well, I say that loosely of course; as much as anyone can keep order when you're faced with hundreds of obstacles. Another favour he asked was very sad. It started from a story about his father. He said he had wonderful memories of his dad being the controller at the level crossing in West Bergholt. In fact, it was between Bergholt and Lexden, in a place called Chitts Hill.

He told me how during the war, the previous controller was having a bath and survived a bomb blast just a few metres away. It was a full-time job and on site was a little cottage; a proper home from home, he called it. I went on to tell him how it hasn't changed and how I often get stuck there when I'm dropping Alice's friend off in Bergholt. So anyway, I went down there and took a photograph for him. When I gave it to him he was very grateful but it stirred up a lot of emotion. I offered to drive him there but he said the photograph was enough and that he would always treasure it.

I carried on going there for another year. Claire even went to the vets for him when his dog was poorly. To be honest, I never thought it ever looked well! Soon after, the dog was put down, and a few months later sadly Brian passed away. I'm so glad I took his garden on and apart from the loss of his dog I hope I contributed to some happiness toward the end of his life.

Since I have been gardening for the past fifteen years I have met some amazing people, from all walks of life. I feel lucky to have worked for them and privileged to have listened to their life stories. One of my old ladies actually fled from occupied Poland during the Second World War. She told me how she and her sister followed rivers and scavenged for food and always managed to avoid the Nazis. I had two more customers that were land girls and two old boys called Vivien; one a chairman of a football club and the other a proper James Herriot vet in the Yorkshire Dales. I have also been to a hundredth birthday party for dear old Nell. She ended her days in a grand old house called Abberton Manor. This is quite a touching story; have you ever heard of a henpecked Tortoise? One of my original customers, Mrs Clark from Mersea Island had this Tortoise called Terry. She said that she found him on the railway line when she lived in London just after the war, which would have made him very old, even for a Tortoise. On regular occasions when I was going round there only to cut the grass I ended up spending half my time looking for Terry. She used to shout, "Terry, where are you," and expect him to come scurrying back like a trained dog, but Terry always hid behind the shrubs and never obeyed her call. I was often confused who I felt sorry for, Terry for getting it in the neck or Mrs Clark for the constant searching. Sometimes I'd spot Terry behind the bushes but keep it to myself. He would look at me in a way only a male to another male would understand, if you get my meaning. One day though it was definitely Mrs Clark I felt so sorry for. Completely distressed, she said she had just had an oil delivery and the man must have over-filled the tank. I guess he was in a hurry because when I turned up the oil had dripped all over Terry's hutch. I tried to mop up as much as I could but it was everywhere. I ended up ringing the oil company and speaking to the manager, who, I have to say, was very obliging. The reason why it was so bad is the oil had actually been delivered over a week ago and unfortunately that was the start of her dementia. The final outcome was a brand new hutch for

Terry, but poor Mrs Clark deteriorated rapidly and eventually went into a home. I don't know what happened to Terry but hopefully he found some peace and quiet. I have lost a lot of customers through dementia and I have seen the heart-ache that the poor relatives go through. I do hope we find a cure and find it soon.

To lighten the mood, one of the funniest moments I had with a customer was when I'd finished cutting her hedge and she wanted to pay me by cheque. She was a retired school teacher and well into her nineties. She was confined to her chair and on this particular day Michelle, the home help nurse, was in the kitchen with her. I used to bump into Michelle quite a lot on Mersea Island, especially on a wet day. I would often pop into the second-hand shop when it was pouring down with rain, you never know what you may find; most of the time it was Michelle! She has a calmness and serenity about her. A trait that is very handy when dealing with the elderly. Michelle was making Mrs C some soup and I was asked to step inside. She had her cheque book ready and asked me the amount and who to make it payable to. I knew she was a bit deaf and she often had trouble with her hearing aid. It used to sound like a whistling kettle and often it would remind me of the feedback you sometimes hear when listening to a live band. Anyway she asked me to spell my name, even though I told her it was the same as the supermarket. I always raised my voice when I spoke to her but I think she was having one of those days with her hearing aid. Realising this, I decided to go up another notch, much to the amusement of Michelle. So I began to spell out each letter; S-A-I- and so on, only Mrs C was really struggling to hear me.

"Pardon?" she said

So I raised my voice even more.

"What," she said, "E?"

"No, I," I said. "I."

"Pardon?"

"I," I repeated.

"E?" she said.

"No, I."

Even the serene Michelle was giggling uncontrollably in the corner. I was desperately trying to hold it together and this went on for a further five minutes! In the end I was shouting like the town crier. It all became too much for Michelle and she had to leave the room. Poor Mrs C soldiered on, repeatedly asking me to spell out my name, completely unaware that Michelle and I were wetting ourselves. I don't know about Mrs C but I came out of there exhausted! A signed blank cheque would have been a hell of a lot easier.

One of the most talented customers I've had, and still have, is a fabulous artist. I helped him a while back with an exhibition at London's City Airport. Painting is more of a hobby to him but he does sell them to raise money for good causes. He's also been given the freedom of the City of London for his services to industry. I'm proud to say I have one of his pictures; it's of a Sri-Lankan bull elephant and it hangs in my living room.

I don't want to turn this into 'confessions of a gardener' but I have to tell you about the most embarrassing time I had on the job. I was cutting a hedge on Mersea Island in the autumn and desperately needed the toilet. The public toilets down on the front are only open during the summer season, which meant I had to ask my customer. When I think back to that day, I'm sure it would have been a lot less hassle to have driven all the way home and all the way back again. The customer was a mother and daughter. I never knew what happened to the dad; in fact, considering they were two of my original clients I didn't know much about them at all, only that they were incredibly private. The daughter, I'm afraid to say, reminded me of Kathy Bates from the film *Misery*. She dressed very dowdily with not a scrap of make-up. The mum was riddled with arthritis and confined to the armchair like Mrs C. The bungalow was caught up in a time-warp, as were the mother and daughter. The garden was straightforward; a grass cut once a fortnight and an annual cut-back of hedges and shrubs. Even though the daughter was about my age and the one who paid me, she hardly ever spoke a word to me. I'm sure she never had a boyfriend; you could just tell because of her behaviour and her awkwardness around me. Even when I tried to make conversation it was always cut short with her looking all Lady Di, twiddling her hair and getting all fidgety before walking off. To begin with, I thought she was rude, but I soon realised she was extremely uncomfortable around anyone other than her mother.

So I knocked on the back door and stepped in. The mum always sat in her armchair in the kitchen. I asked her if I could use her toilet and she obliged. I walked very speedily – like you do when you're desperate for a number two. I got to the bathroom and bolted the door behind me. If I'm totally honest I never felt completely safe round there and I often felt like I was being watched. I don't mean in a sinister way; actually, I do mean in a sinister way. I think I may have watched too many horror movies! All I can say is, I felt a whole lot safer with a hedge-trimmer in my hands but that would have looked a bit weird carrying one of those into the toilet. Anyhow I was dancing around in Kathy Bates's bathroom trying to undo my belt when I noticed the toilet had scaffolding round it. It was one of those commode type thingies. I've seen them before but this one was different. I pondered briefly whilst un-zipping my trousers and came to the conclusion of moving it to one side. Only when I tried to move the damn thing it wouldn't budge; it was fixed to the bloody wall! That certainly proved their lack of visitors. Even more bizarre was the height of the blooming thing. For short people, sitting on it would mean their feet wouldn't even touch the floor! So now my overactive imagination is totally running away with its self. Not only was I trying to have a ---- in Kathy Bates's house but she also keeps a GIANT locked in the cellar! Was it the dad? Now I really am -------- myself! Like I said, the place was in a time-warp, TV and radio hadn't reached these parts and it was quieter than a flipping library. If I sat on it they were going to hear everything! Busting to go and now doing the highland jig I set about trying to dismantle it, but soon realised the bolts were all rusty. I gave it a wiggle but then the tiles starting to lift! No – no, I thought; this was fast becoming my worst nightmare and I was getting very hot and bothered. Then to compound my MISERY Kathy Bates's mum shouted, "Are you OK in there?" Oh no, she's heard me! This was horrendous. Completely mortified and still desperate to go, I thought if I layer the bottom of the pan with toilet roll it might deaden the sound. I sat down and honestly you could have heard a pin drop. I proceeded with my ablutions, coughing all the way – escaping any humiliation, UNTIL – cue Psycho music; I opened the door and found the daughter standing there in the hallway. I leapt out of my bloody skin!

"Are you OK?" she said.

"Yes, fine thank you," I said in a sped-up voice and rushed outside to safety. Why did she pick that moment to speak to me? And why was she standing outside the bathroom? I let them go when I got the school job; surprise, surprise.

One thing I miss about my customers is not having the time anymore for cuppa and a chat. They have so many stories to tell and experiences to share. If people just took a small amount of time in the day to talk and listen to the older generation, they would realise what they have to offer. Some of them used to get out their best china and even bake cakes for me; I used to get proper spoilt! You could tell the ones who were really lonely and it was heart-breaking. I have had too many customers with dementia and I'm convinced that if they had regular interaction with people, their condition might not have accelerated.

Back on the ward; we have had breakfast and the physios are back. They start with getting Jon out of bed. They turn up with crutches for him but of course he's already got some. He picked them up from his surgery and I have to say they are the flashiest crutches I have ever seen. He must have been on that TV program – Pimp My Crutch! Have you ever seen crutches with reflectors before? Obviously they're for getting around safely in the dark. I do believe I've got crutch envy. They get Jon up on his feet; so at least now he can make it to the toilet, which means he won't need the Penis Shy Trap anymore; result!

They work on Pete for a bit before coming to me. I had to tell them about last night and the fact I didn't use the CPM for half of it. They seemed very sympathetic and said if you can, try to use it again. I suppose I will but if I'm going home later, what's the point? They checked I had sufficient movement in my knee before getting me out of bed. It sure felt good to be up but before I can go anywhere I have to get padded up. "Cover your ears everyone, the straps are stuck together." I'm going to end up with perforated ear drums before I get out of here! I slowly but surely make it round to the toilet, so now I won't need the PST; result! I return and they tell me they are pleased with my progress. They also said they will be back later to tackle the stairs. Having had two arthroscopies I'm used to crutches; so about every half hour I was up, even showing off a little at my prowess on two sticks. Hope I don't bump into PC Kemmit! Actually he could be an inspector by now; I don't want to upset him, I'm broken enough! I get back to my bed and take off the cricket pad, plug myself into the CPM like a good boy, and start to dream about getting better. When I do get better I'm not going to go mad; I say to myself I will be more than happy just to have a round of golf again. I joined Colchester Golf Club over ten years ago, but recently I only pay a yearly social membership of about £120. It basically means I can play for a reduced green fee, so long as a seven-day member can sign me in. I've carried it on for years, ever since I couldn't play regularly. If you don't, and want to become a seven day member again, you have to pay the whopping joining fee of over a £1000!

After I broke my leg in my late twenties I took up golf along with my friend Ada. We played every week in a four-ball with Phil and Gordon; both experienced golfers. We had such a laugh. Every Saturday morning we would take it in turns to drive to Gosfield Lake Golf Club. Our old school friend Richard was the golf professional there. I remember saying, long before reality TV shows took off, wouldn't it be a great idea to have a film crew follow us around on the course? Honestly, the banter was second to none and sometimes we could even hit the ball!

My claim to fame was winning an amateurs' major one year. It was the Captain's Day Trophy; one of the biggest events in the club's calendar. After nine holes I knew I was having a good round but never imagined I would keep it going. We popped into the half-way tent where you could have refreshments. As I wasn't driving that day I had a couple of glasses of sparkling wine; It must have really loosened me up because I went on to have my best-ever round of golf. When we finished the buzz got around that I might be in the running. Having my young son William at the time being looked after by my in-laws and Claire away on a bank course, I had to make my excuses not to rush back. I'd been given the all clear by my wonderful in-laws and then Richard fitted me out in a club tie and a blazer from the pro shop. All I was told was that I was in the top three, right up until they announced it. The press were there and the club captain presented me with the trophy, along with a crystal bowl to keep. A couple of weeks later my name was up on the honours board. It was a memorable day.

The golf was also a great way to get the lads together. I'm lucky that I still see a lot of my school friends today, and because I have such a small family, most of them came to our wedding. Most school friends lose contact but we have always made the effort to keep in touch. When we were all getting married off one by one, there was one stag weekend after another.

I have to tell you about the stag weekend in Bath. I was best man for our friends Ada & Sam back in '93; remember Ada's the one who had a brush with death after his hair caught alight. I organised for the lads to stay in a big grand hotel in the middle of Bath, called Pratts would you believe! When we got down there we dumped our bags and got straight on the beer. After a few hours of drinking we found ourselves outside the weir on the river. For whatever reason, Wol and Charlie decided to strip down to their underpants and wrestle one another, sumo style! Well, you should have seen it.

In fact you can, cos one of the lads had a chuck-away camera, it's just a shame he didn't take the photo from the other side because you would have seen the crowd of spectators.

The next bit is the best; within minutes an open top bus pulled up full of Japanese tourists. Instead of taking photos of the beautiful river they turned their cameras toward the wrestling match. Bearing in mind sumo is their national sport, we were sure they'd be offended, but the pair of them actually got a round of applause! Then to cap it all Wolly, who incidentally was my best man, ran over to the bus, grabbed the microphone and said, "That was for Ada and the Tiptree boys," then got more applause. Unbelievable! The whole thing was hilarious and we still talk about it today.

The fact that we have all known each other for so long means there is always a great memory, or a great story to share. When the stag weekends dried up, golf was a great excuse to get away for the weekend. We have had some great times and played some great courses. The last two family holidays I've had have been on golf complexes in Portugal. They offer fantastic facilities and it seems to be the only time I get to play. The beauty of it is you can go round in a buggy and don't have to walk the course. Oh, and the warm sunshine helps the old bones, of course.

Back on the ward, and funny enough the subject turns to sport. Pete's neighbour, who's had a knee replacement, says he owes it to too much cycling. "But I thought cycling was really good for you; no impact on your knees," Jon says.

The problem, he says, is he used to belong to a club and they wouldn't think twice about cycling a hundred miles in one day. He says the bikes then weren't like modern bikes and he used to constantly get out of the saddle and rock the bike from side to side. "Eventually it takes its toll on your knee joints," he says. He also reckons he will be back next year to have the other knee done. Well, you learn something every day; like Jon, I thought cycling was one of the best things for you. I think I'll take up swimming when I get out of here!

Lunch time arrives and once again I have a sandwich and once again they have run out of brown bread. Do they actually have brown bread in hospital? Are you going to tell me that brown bread's not good for me now?! What is the world coming to? Looking at Pete's shepherd's pie, I wish I'd chosen that. At least I've got the fruit pots; I could live on those things. Shane McShane's mum turns up to take him home. Jon and I thought she was his girlfriend; she looks far too young to be a mum, let alone a mum to a seventeen-year-old.

I get up after lunch and go for a little walk on my crutches. I go as far as the staircase – I just wanted to see if I could take them on. Yeah – no problem, I thought. When you have the cricket pad on, your leg is rigid and feels supported. The main problem is, you have to lift your leg from the hip and the hip area has given me the most grief. I'm sure I'll be OK; I desperately want to prove I can do it, so that I can go home later. I make my way back to the ward, thinking about the challenge ahead. There are now two spare beds on the ward; we all seem pretty comfortable and we're all capable of going to the toilet standing up. Not a PST in sight! At least Gladys and Keira get a bit of a break; god knows they deserve it. Mind you, they'll only have to start all over again when the next lot arrive. Time moves slowly for the next hour or two. Jon and I talk about meeting up for a drink and a curry when we get out.

Before you know it the physios are back and it's time to tackle the stairs – two guys this time and the topic turns to football straight away. I tell them that my leg problems first occurred after I broke my leg playing for Tiptree Heath. He starts talking about seeing Colchester's great escape on the last day of the season. How one minute he thought they were staying up, then going down, and then how they managed to avoid relegation right at the death. The other physio happened to play against my son in a semi-final just three weeks ago.

We get to the staircase and the physios show me the technique of holding the crutch in the same hand, next to the one you're using. That way you have your spare when you reach the top. It's a technique I have to master, otherwise they won't let me go home. I'm thrilled to say I pass the staircase challenge and make my way back to the ward. Jon could tell by the look on my face that I was one step closer to going home. He hasn't got to do the staircase challenge because he's going to sleep downstairs.

Keira checks my blood pressure and takes my temperature, probably for the last time. "I hear you are just about ready to go," she says.

"Yeah, all I need now is for Gladys to knock me up a goody bag," I reply.

"Well, good luck with everything," she says.

This is the moment I've been waiting for. I do feel a bit guilty, though, because she's been fine all day, but then again

I can't let an opportunity slip by. Gladys has got her mobile sweet trolley and she's coming my way. It just so happens she's going to change the dressing on my hip. The dressing on the leg needs to stay on for a further two weeks and must be kept dry. However the dressing on the donor site, situated between my groin and hip, needs replacing. Gladys pulls the curtains round and I seize the moment. First thing I have to do is butter her up; so I ask her how her afternoon is going and if she goes to church. I know it sounds a bit random but bear with (now I sound like Miranda).

"Yes. Why?" she says.

"I heard you singing to yourself, that's all; was it gospel?"

"Mm," she mutters and seems a bit embarrassed. She pulls the top dressing off carefully, mainly because of its position. Underneath is a skin-like dressing. That one is a bit stickier and requires my help. It is a bit like a waxing; I am pushing down on my skin while she is ripping off my hairs. She is gentle, though, I have to say. I'd given Jon the wink before Gladys pulled round the curtains, so he knows I am up to something. He must have put his finger to his lips to warn the other two, because the ward becomes deathly silent. Perfect – now for my Carry On moment; I promise not to say Ooh Matron!

As soon as both dressings are off you can see the wound. It has been stapled; about a dozen in all. Shamelessly I say to her, "What do you think then, is it bigger than you thought?"

Disappointingly she replies: "No, it's about average." You can sense the ears pricking up.

I respond with, "Oh, that's a shame; I was hoping you were going to say it's the biggest one you have ever seen."

"Well I suppose it is a good size," she says and then the lads roar with laughter. Gladys, to her credit, realises what she's said and a big grin appears on her face. She puts the new dressing on, shakes her head and says, "Naughty naughty, you are very naughty." She pulls the curtains back and there is Jon, laughing his head off. I feel a little rotten, but then again she was a bit rotten to me yesterday.

Before you know it, it's visiting time again. Pete and the guy next to him have family visiting; Jon unfortunately has to wait till later for a friend to pick him up. I did offer Claire to take him home, but I don't think he wants to trouble anyone. My mum and dad visit and I tell them about my saga last night; more sympathy! They are glad to see me having a better day and shocked to hear that I am going home. I think mum worries I'm going to overdo it; you know what mum's can be like. She sees how hard I hit the gardening and fears that I will try to run before I can walk. I am a bit impatient but assure her that I will be more than happy just to go for a stroll when I'm back to normal. They have a Jack Russell and enjoy walking her every day. At the moment walking the dog seems very appealing. I tell them not to hang around and that Claire will come and get me. They give me a hug and promise to visit me in a couple of days when I'm home.

Gladys comes back wearing a big beaming smile and hands me my goody bag. I'm not sure if she's smiling because of what happened earlier, or she's just so happy to see the back of me; either way we had a bit of a giggle, and I'm just glad to see her smiling; she has a lovely smile. Gladys gives me the news I've been waiting for. I shake her hand and off she goes. I take a peek into my goody bag; no sherbet dib-dab, no penny chews; not even a toy, just dihydrocodeine, paracetamol, Senna and a couple of dressings; never mind… I read the note, put it back in the bag and put the bag into my ruck-sack. I pick up my phone and ring Claire. "I'm ready to come home, see you in a little while." I'm so lucky to have a wife like Claire; we had our 25th wedding anniversary last year. I love her so much and I know she will look after me.

Six in the evening and Claire walks in; she gives me a kiss and asks if I'm ready. "You bet," I say. She gathers my stuff together, says goodbye to the others and thanks the nurses. She then helps me to my feet and then goes off to collect the car. The hospital charges for parking, but personally I have never used it. I always park in a quiet cul-de-sac five minutes away.

Well, it's time to say my goodbyes. I wish the fellas well and make a special effort to shake Jon's hand. We both agree to meet up in future and off I go. I stop to thank Keira and Gladys for looking after me, and make my way out of the Great Tey Plaza. I was lucky to have Jon as a pal and the other guys were great too. The nurses as always were brilliant. The consultant has done a great job (well, I hope he has). I haven't got an infection; I have been fed (shame about the white bread but the fruit pots made up for it) and I'm walking out of here in one piece. My hospital might still be under review but I survived it. I can't say it wasn't painless because of my little episode but bearing in mind I had surgery in two different places, I don't think I did badly. I only had one night's stay and I believe I had the best possible care. So I'd like to say a huge THANK YOU to Colchester General Hospital… You are all wonderful.

Now I was going to end it here apart from some local history about Tiptree but the next part is hilariously gross, at my expense of course. I have to warn you though, I'm giving you a warts-and-all account and it's not for the faint hearted! I will pick it up where we left off.

Claire picks me up first and then Alice, who was staying at a friend's house in Bergholt. We stop off at a local fast food restaurant before reaching home about 8.30pm. It is good to be home and it is hard to believe I was only in for one night; it seemed a lot longer. Alice wants to know what I've bought home. "Nothing exciting," I say, "just the cricket pad, pain killers, dressings and some laxatives."

She asks me how often I have to take them and I tell her the pain killers every day but the laxatives only when you need to. When you get to my age you know your own body, so I think I will probably not need the laxatives (big mistake!). Nobody in hospital said take them anyway, to stop you getting constipated. The thing is you don't feel that hungry in hospital and the fact that I haven't been to the toilet doesn't even cross my mind. So with no feeling of constipation, just discomfort in the hip and groin area, I settle down to a first night in my own bed. Lovely – you can't beat your own bed. The hardest thing for me is not being able to lie on my side. I get up two or three times in the night to go for a wee, each time having to put on the cricket pad (god, that Velcro is loud!). I even try to leave it on for a while but it makes me too hot; best option is to leave it off and eventually I do get back to sleep.

WEDNESDAY: Claire and William go off to work and Alice goes to school. Alice makes sure I have everything I need so I don't have to climb the stairs. Knowing all about rehab and the importance of doing ones exercises, I set about being a good boy. Claire comes home for lunch and then I get a visit from her mum and dad. Claire's dad John tells me how Gladys was the Staff Nurse when he was in hospital a few years back, after a hip replacement. We have fish and chips for tea and an early night. I still haven't gone for a number two, but I am not too worried. I wake up in the middle of the night in a lot of pain from the hip area and have to take some extra painkillers. THURSDAY: (not such a good day) Claire nips home for lunch but then goes off to college all afternoon and evening and I am expecting no more visitors. As much as my hip and groin are painful, I still feel like I need to stretch or do something. Maybe I am missing the CPM after all. I am getting up mega early, which makes the day really long and arduous, although writing this book has helped enormously with the boredom.

Thursday afternoon and all of a sudden, the pain in my hip has reached tipping point. I stock up on painkillers and crawl up stairs to bed, hoping it will wear off. Half an hour later and I am beside myself with pain. I'd say after living with pain for quite a few years now that my threshold is pretty high, but this is nearing towards the Monday night episode. Realising that lying in bed made no difference, I then struggle back down stairs. The pain killers are not making any impression and just like Monday night I have got myself into a position of no return. The sensation is hard to describe, but if you can imagine your hip is trapped in a vice and someone is winding it tighter and tighter; that's how it feels. I try to sit on the sofa but the slightest movement sends me into lockdown. So then I try planting my good leg, knee bent on the sofa and my bad leg straight to the floor, but end up with my bum stuck in the air. If you happen to look through the window at the time you would think I am twerking in slow-motion; very badly! You may laugh but it's like having permanent cramp; you dare not move. Just at that point Alice walks through the door. She asks what's wrong and I try to explain, but I can hardly string a sentence together. She just about understands my stuttering and knows that I am in desperate need of something stronger. Morphine is the only thing that worked in hospital and that's exactly what I need right now. Between us we manage to contact the surgery. I feel like a crazed crack head waiting for his next fix! So off she goes, bless her – in the pouring rain. Luckily the surgery is only a five-minute walk, and she soon comes back with the prescription. She then phones Nan and Grandad Lambs to come over and take the prescription to the drive-through Boots. About forty-five minutes later I am getting high on morphine. If Alice had not turned up when she did I think I might have passed out. John and Jean stick around until I am comfortable and were just great. As soon as they left I get an unexpected visit from my friend Ada. It is good to see him but the timing isn't perfect. He stops for about five minutes and then says he'll drop by next week when I am feeling better. I feel terrible for him, but mainly for Alice seeing her dad in that state, and desperately hope whatever it is that caused it will never return.

FRIDAY: the end of the week cannot come soon enough and once Friday is over I can be with my lovely family all weekend. Mum and dad pop over for lunch, which is nice, and I tell them about yesterday and how their wonderful granddaughter saved the day. I am still doing my exercises three or four times a day, but after not doing a number two all week, I think it wise to start taking the Senna tablets (laxatives). I'm not in any pain down there but I am getting slightly concerned, especially given the fact I'm normally so regular.

SATURDAY: the weekend I was looking forward to turns into my worst nightmare!

I wake up feeling OK, but I can't get used to sleeping on my back. It's so unnatural; I feel like I'm lying in a coffin and I can't wait to roll onto my side, that's when I'm most comfortable. Because of the rain on Thursday the grass has been growing like mad so Claire and William are hoping to go grass cutting this morning. Looks like a good day for it, I thought. If only I could go with them, I could start the mowers and see my customers. At least I would be doing something useful. I hate not helping and when I look outside and see the grass growing I just think I could be earning. I doubt I will be grass cutting for quite a long time yet. I will have to be patient and keep doing my exercises. It is past breakfast time and Claire and William are getting ready to go; I, on the other hand, have (thank goodness) finally got the urge to do a No 2. I can hear William asking his mum what mowers to take. I have four, so I shout from the downstairs toilet which two to put on the van. There – I do have my uses. Claire makes up a snack and a couple of drinks and says, "See you later and don't forget you have Nurse Alice if you need anything."

The moment she stepped out the door, I yelled, "You're not going anywhere."

"Why not?" She replied.

"Because I'm trying to poo and it won't come out," I said.

"Just push a bit harder," was Claire's response.

Well, I'm sure you are not interested in my ablutions, especially after the Kathy Bates story, but I have never had to push hard in my life! Claire literally was about to leave and I started to panic. The pain was cranking up and I could not imagine being left with poor Alice to nurse a pathetic creature like dad again, so I cried, "Stop."

"Well, how bad is it?" asked Claire.

"Really bad," I groaned. "In fact, I think you need to call someone."

"Oh," she said, "Who?"

"I don't know, a doctor – nurse – plumber – anyone who can help, 'cos it ain't moving."

Not knowing what it's like to be constipated and now deeply regretting not taking the Senna daily after leaving hospital, I now find myself in an even worse situation than Thursday. The feeling is quite overwhelming. After feeling nothing all week, I suddenly feel like I'm about to give birth to a baby elephant! I have the sensation of passing the biggest poo ever, but I also feel like someone has sadistically stitched up my passage. It's like a huge glacier shifting slowly through a blocked up tunnel. It feels like something is about to burst, like my eyes could actually pop out. The pain is intolerable. After quick consideration, my wonderful wife Claire decides to call the NHS walk-in centre. She speaks to a nurse who tells her to examine the patient and report back. In other words, look up my back side! You know you truly love someone when a complete stranger asks you to peer up your partner's bum hole. I hear Claire say to the nurse, "Really?" I can see the look of horror on her face. I even notice her lips curling up as I manoeuvre myself round for her to examine me. There I am bent over clutching the rim of the pan, while my teenage sweetheart tells the nurse in great detail what she can see. "No gaps – I can see the poo but everything looks very tight and painfully stretched." Humiliation complete! She may as well be saying, "He's fully dilated – the poo is stuck and we need to operate!" Like Alan Bennett said in his film *The Lady in The Van*, 'Caring is about shit'. I think to myself, is this one of those crystal ball moments where you can see into the future? I'm not sure I want to get old!

The nurse goes on to say, "Can you get him here?" and Claire replies, "We're on our way." Cricket pad on and crutches at the ready, it is time to go. The distance from the downstairs toilet to the car is about three metres, but it takes me about ten minutes and I am sweating like a pig. Every step I take I think I'm going to shit myself, which is ironic really because that's exactly what I want. God, I hate gravity right now; I just want to float there without sitting down.

Getting into the car is proving to be so difficult you wouldn't believe it. I hold onto the roof of the car and gently ease myself down, hovering above the seat. I'm attempting a one legged squat and I can't help thinking if I collapse onto the seat it will only push it back up there, or worse snap off like a chair leg. I then manage to grip hold of the handle with my left hand and with the other, push myself up like a one-handed press up. Every muscle in my body is screaming and my left thigh is burning like crazy. Am I going to make it? It's bad enough travelling with a fresh wound to my leg and groin, but to throw in a gargantuan poo sticking out my arse is taking the biscuit! To say it's the longest journey of my life is an understatement. I've been on a plane to Australia and it was a breeze compared to this! When I get out the other end, I'm going to look like a really crap Cossack dancer!

Claire pulls the car up outside the main entrance and helps me out. Boy was that good to get out; god knows how I held on to that position, and it was such a relief to stretch out my left leg. I can see her parking not too far away so I begin at snail's pace to enter the building. Claire soon passes me and I follow like an old relative. She goes to the front desk and I'm desperately thinking to myself, please be seen, please be seen. People are looking at me and wondering why I'm not sitting down. I then get panicky and wonder if people can actually smell it? I keep asking Claire if she can smell me but she says I am being paranoid and then reassures me, it won't be long. I am shifting around on my crutches, perspiring, breathing heavily and in a great deal of discomfort. It is so obvious I'm in agony and people begin to really stare. Do you ever do that thing in waiting rooms where you try to guess people's ailments? I just want to put everyone's curiosity to rest and shout, "OK everyone, guess what – I have a huge poo sticking out of my arse – so there, guessing over!"

The nurse came out and called my name, thank god, and we both go in. She doesn't waste any time and tells me to remove my trousers and lie on the bed. She tells us to be patient while she hunts around the room for a box of enemas. When she finds the box, there are only two left. Bizarrely she then asks Claire if she would like to administer one. Claire, with yet another look of horror on her face, swiftly responds with an emphatic NO THANK YOU! The nurse then tells me to lie on my side and before I can say '*All Creatures Great and Small*' she shoots the enema up my backside! It makes me go boss-eyed and then immediately wonder why anyone would choose to pay for colonic irrigation. She then tells me to rush to the toilet and expect the inevitable. I get up and dash as fast as any person you may have seen wearing a splint, on crutches, with a poo poking out of their arse! She follows behind and waits outside like an expectant father. Several minutes later I am still inside the unlocked toilet, huffing and puffing, trying to breathe into my contractions. "Are you OK in there?" she says. Oh god it's like Cathy Bates all over again!

"No," I cry, "I don't think it's worked."

"Come on then, out you come."

All it has done is give my poo a wash and a rinse and fill my backside with water, so now I have the added humiliation of dribbling my way back to her room for another examination. I clamber up onto the bed feeling as feeble as ever, and she shoots another round of liquid up my bum. "This better work," she says, "that was the last one." I feel like I've been bitten by a snake and now they've run out of anti-venom!

I go back to the loo, but there is no poo! I told you I write poetry. By now I feel like a magnum of champagne with the cork half off; the pressure is building and I am worried I am going to take someone's eye out! The nurse looks dejected and I look even more so.

The next course of action is to go home with two sachets of laxatives. I thank her and comically we both apologise to one another. She seems genuinely gutted she couldn't finish the job (pardon the pun).

As you can imagine, the journey home is equally as bad and I am hoping to make it back without re-upholstering the car.

We manage to get home without incident and I immediately take the laxative. Feeling weak, despondent and with a backside like Mount Vesuvius, the only thing to do is to wait. The whole morning has passed by and poor Claire cannot make any plans for the afternoon, because she is on standby. The parallels to being in labour are uncanny, apart from the end bit of course.

I spend the next couple of hours straining, groaning and aching with pain. It is like some sort of torture, having to be glued to the toilet seat, and I feel as vile as Jabba the Hutt sitting in his palace. Just when I think matters can't get any worse, I surrender myself to an act of degradation. I prise my bum off the toilet seat, stand up and run a basin full of hot steamy water. By now I am absolutely desperate and in the back of my sordid mind, I know exactly what I want to do. Somehow I manage to stand up on the side of the bath with my good leg and manoeuvre the other leg (still in the splint) over the basin and onto the lid of the toilet. I must look like one those camping tripods, with the pot (my bum) dangling over the fire. One slip and I could plunge into my makeshift bidet! It is a risky move, granted – but for a brief moment I sigh with relief as the steam soothes my backside.

I stay there with my bum suspended above the basin until the water is cool enough to break the surface. It is the nearest thing I have to a birthing pool and I am running out of options. The basin cups my sore, taut bottom and the warm water caresses my bum cheeks. I sigh once more. It's like one those macabre Japanese game shows, and after a couple of minutes I peer between my outstretched legs like a yoga warrior. The once clear water has now turned to a muddy brown and I know at that moment, it is time to strike. I cannot suffer it any longer and I do the unthinkable.

Now battling against the cramp, I begin to claw my way into my backside like I am banishing an evil spirit. Mixed with the warm water, my poo is like clay between my fingers, but it was never going look like the scene from Ghost. I even contemplate shouting to Claire to go and fetch a cocktail spoon! Anything to get this entity out of me! I know it's disgusting and utterly deplorable, but I did warn you! All in all, I think, I only manage to scrape the surface but at least I have broken off the bit that was sticking out. I clean myself up as best I can but inside I feel as dirty as hell.

I admit to Claire what I have done, like a bad catholic in a confessional and then crash out on the bed. I am exhausted and distraught that my hideous sordid plan didn't work. Claire has been great throughout and keeps checking up on me. I honestly think that the laxatives are not going to work. I feel like I am going to be stuck like this forever!

It must be reaching late afternoon and I start to get really hot, like I am running a temperature. I drift off and then I must have called out to Claire, because she says I am in a state of delirium and I wake up in a pool of sweat. She is very concerned and calls the walk-in centre straight away. They say they will send out a district nurse as soon as possible. Claire gets a shock when she arrives, it's only the same nurse!

She says she is here to finish the job, and I am just glad it's one less person looking up my backside. I can hear her talking to Claire about something, probably because I am in no fit state to communicate. She comes into the bedroom and says that I have severe faecal impaction, and would it be OK to give me another colonic injection?

To be honest, she could have taken my tonsils out for all I cared, anything to put me out of my misery. I just nod for her to get on with it. I soon come out of my state of delirium though, when she produces the biggest syringe I have ever seen! Surely not, I think; she really does think she's James Herriot this time! Once again – as quick as a flash I am on my side and she empties the lot up my derriere. This time it's like having a hosepipe up there and I don't even want to think about what it must be like for her. After going boss-eyed once more, I then apologise for wetting the bed but she tells me that I haven't, and it is just a similar sensation. She says, "Up you get, and get to that toilet quick."

I think she is expecting results, and I can hear her say to Claire that if it doesn't work, it will have to be done surgically. With the fear of possible surgery looming, I am even more determined to get rid of this bloody poo. The noise coming from our bathroom must have been heard a block away! I reckon I must have been in there straining for about fifteen to twenty minutes before I finally give birth to an ugly six-pounder! The feeling of euphoria was overwhelming and, like any father, I cried my eyes out. I know it's wrong to liken my experience to giving birth, because how would I know? All I can say is – I have even more respect for first-time mums and if I end up with stretch marks, then so be it! Without sounding too corny, the district nurse has finally done her job, because I have done mine. Claire and I cannot thank her enough. Like I said before – those nurses are real life angels and she was the best; I will be eternally indebted.

So there you have it, my time in hospital and a week convalescing – if you can call it that! Lessons learnt – be good to your partner, you might need them to peer up your backside! If you ever have an operation, make sure you take your constipation tablets every day, and finally, remember what a wonderful job the staff do every single day in our fantastic NHS.

If you lived or indeed live in Tiptree, you will recognise a lot of the photos at the end of the book. I really struggled to find photos from the '70s to the '80s relating to Tiptree. The ones I have I will share with you, and the rest are photos I have taken recently. The next image is an old, rather crude map of Tiptree and all the roads I have lived in. The Anchor Press has been replaced by one of the big supermarkets, and the railway track is now a housing estate. The big chunk of land to the right of the park has also turned into housing. Opposite the cut and The Ducka stands yet another big supermarket. In the '70s it would have been the Carrot Topping Factory and just like the Anchor Press, we would jump into a skip; but instead of reading, we'd be munching our way through our own body weight in carrots!

Next door to the carrot factory was the basket factory. It was owned by Mr Martin, and the family lived in a big house on the same site. Beside the house there was a beautiful green lawn and I have recently found out that my friend Brett used to mow it regularly for pocket money. Flanking the lawn was a beautiful cobnut orchard. I know it was naughty, but we used to fill up a Budgens bag full of nuts and then have a picnic in the roof of his summer house. Next to that used to be the doctor's, and behind the surgery was the dentist. I remember he used to say, "Grab an apple on the way out," and every time I bit into it I'd see blood! Needless to say, he wasn't a very good dentist. Continuing along and across Grove Road was Budgens and the infamous wall. That was the place to hang out.

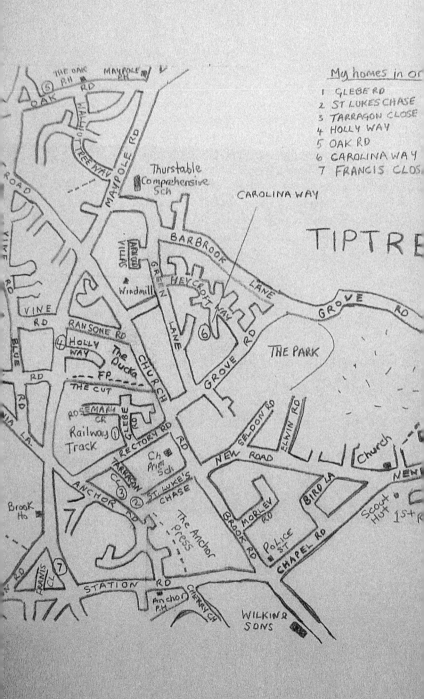

My homes in or

1 GLEBE RD
2 ST LUKES CHASE
3 TARRAGON CLOSE
4 HOLLY WAY
5 OAK RD
6 CAROLINA WAY
7 FRANCIS CLOS

TIPTRE

CAROLINA WAY

THE OAK P.H
MAYPOLE
OAK RD
WALNUT TREE WAY
MAYPOLE RD

Thurstable
Comprehensive
Sch

ROAD

VINE RD

SYLVIA
ARGOW
GREEN LANE

BARBROOK LANE

GROVE RD

Windmill

HEYCROFT WAY

VINE RD

RANSOME RD

BLUE RD

HOLLY WAY

The Ducks

CHURCH LANE

6

GROVE RD

THE PARK

FP

THE CUT

ROSEMARY CR

LA.

Railway Track

1

GLEBE RD

RECTORY RD

NEW SELDON RD

ELWIN RD

Church

RD

NEW ROAD

NEW

Ch
Prim
Sch

TARRAGON CL

3 2 ST LUKE'S CHASE

Brook Ho

ANCHOR RD

7

BROOK RD

MORLEY RD

BIRD LA

Scout Hut 1ST R

The Anchor press

POLICE ST

CHAPEL RD

RD

FRANCIS CL

7

STATION RD

CHERRY CH

Anchor P.H

WILKIN & SONS

Writing this book and harking back to my childhood has brought back so many memories. Since I started talking to people about Tiptree, many have said the same thing; that they are saddened by the number of changes to their village. Wilkin & Sons have finally decided to stay in the village, and I'm so glad the other option to move away didn't happen. Without them, I fear Tiptree would lose its identity; in a village that's already lost the Anchor Press and loved shops like the Kilty Cake shop, Arnolds, Ketley's, Bassinghams, Mr Tooles, the wool shop and many more. Honestly, have you ever heard of a toy shop that sells maggots? – well, Bassinghams did! A wool shop that sold theatre tickets! If you wanted air rifle pellets you didn't go to a gun shop, you went to Crampins Garage, of course. Thank goodness that the Cheap Shop, Staines & Brights (which incidentally used to have a cinema upstairs), Colin's barbers and Brian's hair salon have all survived. I might have moved away but I still have a deep ingrained sentiment about the place I often call 'my giant playground'.

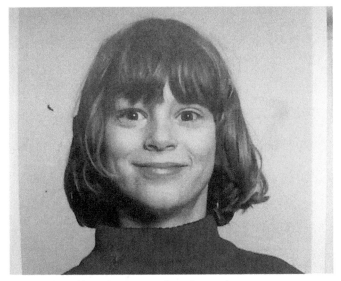

The 'long-haired lover from Liverpool', without a plait.

Playing in the Park', with my friend Mick in 1973.
Grove Road would be outside left of picture.

Giddy up'. Three years after this picture was taken,
I broke my arm on that see-saw!

I found this aerial view of The Anchor Press, kindly donated by Charles Willis (circa 1967) and amazingly it shows a photograph of our flat in St Luke's Chase (centre). It's the only photo I've ever seen of our so-called 'haunted house', and it made me feel quite emotional. To the left are the grounds of my first school – St Luke's. The chase ran between the school and Hutchinson's (part of the Anchor Press), then narrowed into a cut. If you look at the cars parked in a row; at the bottom there's a gap in the trees; that eventually became the back gardens to Tarragon Close, my third home. I reckon my house, No 37, would be in the middle of that brown field. On the far right you can see some new semi-detached houses. The one in the middle became Wol's house. About ten years after this picture was taken, we would have been calling in Gibbon to one another and building dens out of pallets – right where those cars are parked.

House No 3

Above is Tarragon Close today. My house was the one on the right. The path turns left and leads to the cut before opening out to St Luke's Chase. The tall white house and the house next to it would have been the site of our old flat, so you see we didn't have to move very far. To the right of this photo is another cut that leads to Anchor Road. Looking back at the old photo of the Anchor Press, you can just make out a circular concrete reservoir; it's above the lawn – top of picture. That's where I split my head open and ran into the club. The other reservoir must have been built later. St Luke's Chase was also the spot where Dave shot a banger (firework) out of a copper pipe and hit me in the forehead. For weeks, I looked like a Hindu with one of those bindi dots on my forehead!

House No 4

House No 5 - Oak Road

House No 6

House No 7 - Francis Close

The fire station, not a climbing frame!

The old conker tree is still alive (just). It's hard to believe we used to sit up there. 'If only trees could talk', as they say.

The Ducka.

The bush is still there! We used to play football round it.

The Ducka end of Glebe Rd – my first home. The railings in the cut have replaced the original four posts. The posts were a perfect height for sitting tin cans on. This is where Tony split my head open with a jagged bone when I was collecting my ammo.

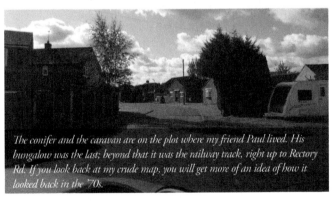

The conifer and the caravan are on the plot where my friend Paul lived. His bungalow was the last; beyond that it was the railway track, right up to Rectory Rd. If you look back at my crude map, you will get more of an idea of how it looked back in the '70s.

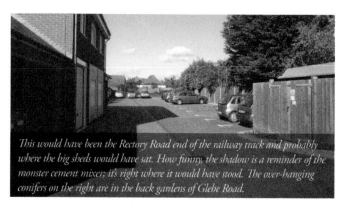

This would have been the Rectory Road end of the railway track and probably where the big sheds would have sat. How funny, the shadow is a reminder of the monster cement mixer; its right where it would have stood. The over-hanging conifers on the right are in the back gardens of Glebe Road.

The park as it is today, taken from Grove Road.

What used to be a convenience shop owned by my friend Pete's parents. It was just the place to buy a penny ice pole.

It's now a housing estate! The following photo shows the Anchor Press, taken from the same spot. The Social Club was to the left and the concrete reservoirs would have been out of picture to the right.

Picket line, probably from 1980.
(Photo kindly donated by Norman Hopkins)

Can't imagine the police driving around in a Mini nowadays!

The building that stands behind the Vauxhall Viva (front left) was the old snooker club. We used to leave the windows unbolted and then go back when everyone went home, shut the curtains and have a free game of snooker. Sorry mum!

Although this wasn't a book of poems and gettin' poetic doesn't mean you have to recite poetry, I still feel a bit of a cheat. After all, I did say I enjoy writing poetry. The short of it is, because I feel a bit guilty, I'd like to share with you a couple of my poems. I'm not that good but I do enjoy writing poetry when I'm in the mood. I guess it's because I'm not particularly eloquent, so writing stuff down helps with expression. Sometimes it's easier for people to articulate feelings in words. Having only written poems for loved ones, friends and work colleagues, where you can dish the dirt or add some comedy, I'd like to write something that has a message. My son William was at a house party which ended in tragedy. He was sixteen at the time, and the horrific events that unfolded made all the national papers and all the major news channels. Every parent's worst nightmare is when the police come knocking on your door. For us, it was to call William in for questioning, but unfortunately for another parent it was the worst possible news: their child had been stabbed to death. I can't imagine the anger and the pain that poor family went through. They did eventually convict the evil person that took away that young boy's life. Knife crime is here, here on our doorstep and we need to stop it! This is my short poem against knife crime.

One blade too many
Blood is like a river running through your vein,
Sometimes the river stops causing lots of pain.
You can tell when a river's healthy it's clean and full of life.
So let our rivers breathe and put away the knife.
RIP Jay Whiston.

I want to end the book on a positive happy note, so my other poem is dedicated to my gorgeous wife Claire. I have to admit, though, it's a bit of a rip off because it contains song titles. I read some of it out at our joint 50th birthday party, and to embarrass her even further I'd like to share it with you. It was supposed to be a sort of quiz, but I stupidly left the first page at home and couldn't quite remember it all. I think I just about managed to pull it off as a lot of the guests were shouting out titles of songs; either that or they were telling me to 'Stand down Margaret'! If you want to play along, it helps if you're of a certain age or into you're '80s music. If your knowledge of '80s music is good, you should get at least 25. You have to picture the scene. I was working for a lifeboat repair company in Tiptree and I used to dash out to catch a glimpse of my sweetheart Claire going home on the bus. The object is to pick out the lyrics, title and artist, so I'll say good luck, goodbye and thank you for reading. It's called Love In The '80s, and if it's no good 'I'll rip it up and start again'! I give away the first artist.

Cast your mind back to the year of '82.

I was mending lifeboats while Hoggy was sniffing glue!

It was a sunny day, in the month of June

Fat Larry's Band on the radio, singing their song ----.

I felt under pressure, a feeling I could not hide.

Time was ticking on, I had to dash outside.

Long before Snapchat, Twitter or download.

It was enough to catch a glimpse of her, passing down the road.

If I missed Claire on her bus, on her way back from sixth form,

I'd sniff a pot of Hoggy's glue and then look all forlorn!

But I would not give in, I kept dashing out, like I was attached to a length of string.

Now it makes all perfect sense, never give up on a good thing.

I was torn, though, between Claire and my mates.

It was a game of push and shove.

But when she said, "Don't you want me?" I knew – it must be love.

There was something about her I could not resist, was it her cute little frown?

Or was it the legs right up to her ears, or her eyes of golden brown!

A couple of parties later I asked her out on Kelvedon bridge.

I tried to play it cool, wearing a mac like Midge!... Ah, Vienna.

She said ge– No, only kidding, she said YES I'll be your girlfriend.

It was such a lovely day.

I was in rapture – the reflex was to shout Enola Gay!

She was my Caribbean Queen, my eye of the tiger, my dead ringer for love.

She was my 9 to 5, my love resurrection, my wings of a dove.

But I nearly lost her.

One day I didn't turn up, was I going insane?

I caught her up, out on her bike in the pouring rain!

She said, "Beat it, you're too footloose and you're living on a prayer."

I told her, "You need to relax, I know it's a sin and you're on the road to nowhere."

She screamed, "You spin me round, you're no Prince Charming, stop looking at me like some lost pup."

I said, "When the going gets tough the tough get going,
Never gonna give you up!"

Sweet Dreams x

Lightning Source UK Ltd.
Milton Keynes UK
UKOW06f2301160917
309299UK00007B/62/P

9 781911 525622